A CENTURY OF THE CATHOLIC CHURCH IN TIVLAND (1921-2021)

A CENTURY OF THE CATHOLIC CHURCH IN TIVLAND (1921-2021)

Gabriel T. Wankar
Moses A. Iorapuu
Joseph Eneji
(Editors)

PAULINES PUBLICATIONS WEST AFRICA

A CENTURY OF THE CATHOLIC CHURCH
IN TIVLAND (1921-2021)

ISBN 978-978-58695-6-9

Year of Publication 2022

PAULINES PUBLICATIONS WEST AFRICA
Daughters of St Paul
Kado Kuchi, ABUJA (NIGERIA)
E-mail: publicationsabuja@gmail.com ; Tel: +2348074794730
www.paulineswestafrica.org

Layout & Cover Oluwakemi Akinleye fsp

Printed by TOTMA PRINT, Lagos

A CENTURY OF THE CATHOLIC CHURCH IN TIVLAND (1921-2021)

Gabriel T. Wankar
Moses A. Iorapuu
Joseph Eneji
(Editors)

PAULINES PUBLICATIONS WEST AFRICA

A CENTURY OF THE CATHOLIC CHURCH
IN TIVLAND (1921-2021)

ISBN 978-978-58695-6-9

Year of Publication 2022

PAULINES PUBLICATIONS WEST AFRICA
Daughters of St Paul
Kado Kuchi, ABUJA (NIGERIA)
E-mail: publicationsabuja@gmail.com ; Tel: +2348074794730
www.paulineswestafrica.org

Layout & Cover Oluwakemi Akinleye fsp

Printed by TOTMA PRINT, Lagos

Contents

Foreword

The somewhat convoluted history of the mission of Christ in Tivland is a tale of hardiness, tenacity, resilience and triumph. The admixture of resistance, curiosity, dilemma and doubt, reluctant acceptance and firebrand fanaticism that makes up the panorama of the Tiv Mission was the product of its early beginnings.

Until the advent of Christianity, the Tiv People lived as a family and practiced a form of communalism that was akin to the values brought by the new religion. Far from a romanticism with the traditions of the Tiv people, one can affirm that the cohesive spirit of the Tiv has been certainly confused by the many brands of Christianity that have inundated Tivland in the past half a century.

As was the case in most other African instances, the advent of Christianity was coeval with the bitter experience of colonisation. Indeed, that contemporaneity posed many challenges the early missionaries had to contend with. As far as the people were concerned, the Christian mission, despite presenting a fascia of peace and non-violence, was that other unknown side of the colonial coin.

In time though, the resistance of the people was overcome. Not so much by the hardiness of the white missionaries per se, but also by the natural curiosity of the people whose initial doubt metamorphosed into a dilemma (torn as it were between the old and the new) and finally to reluctant acceptance. That hesitant acceptance would soon give way to a firebrand fanaticism that made it possible for these people of culture and crystallised customs to have their indigenous priests in the new religion in record time. Although the other Missions had established their presence before the Catholic Church, the ordination of Tiv priests would become a watershed that would transform Tivland.

Thus, over the last hundred years, Christianity has witnessed phenomenal, almost miraculous, growth in Tivland. This is the tale narrated by this tidy collection of articles put together by people who, in one way or the other, are themselves woven into the tapestry of this history. I highly recommend this collection to all.

Most Rev. Wilfred C. Anagbe, cmf
Bishop, Catholic Diocese of Makurdi

Acknowledgements

Though on the Catholic Church in Tivland, these essays are not intended as a theological journal nor a compendium to teach Catholic doctrine. The volume aspires to let the "symphony" of Catholic historical presence among the Tiv resound in its pages – not only for Catholics but also for any person concerned with uniting faith with culture and social transformation.

In recounting the Catholic spiritual heritage among the Tiv and the modest contributions to social development in Tivland from the 1920s to the present, we express our indebtedness to the late Professor David Iornongu Ker, OON, whose persistent prodding catalysed this work.

We are grateful to the Bishops of the Catholic Dioceses in Tivland, whose Dioceses form the study area for the compendium. Importantly, we duly acknowledge the authors whose books and ideas are used by the various authors of the different chapters in this volume. Fathers Dominic Ukan Jir and Clement Akume Mato were valuable informants, as well as Catechist Vincent Tartser of Naka, Baba Vincent Agber Chiawa of Korinya, and Chief Jerome Haa Orpin of Yandev.

Our sincere gratitude belongs to Mr Nathaniel Ikyur, Mary Bordi, Denis Nolan, and Maureen Puchinelli for their time in studying the original script and offering valuable comments and insights. Our support staff provided assistance that went beyond technical – Lyamnger Agir, Jacob Tyokyaa, Godwin Akpough, and Sarah Manzano – we love you all.

Fathers Marcellinus Wendeh, Jacob Ahar, Victor Uvihi, Andrew Atime, James Utav and Pastor Peter Ichull all helped with information gathering, and we are most grateful. Above all, to God be the glory for this modest effort, which is never an exhaustive history but a challenge for others to document and come up with something even better in the future.

Editors

Chapter One

Catholicism and Protestantism in Tivland: Encounters with the NKST, 1921-2021

Iyorwuese Hagher[1]

Background

Tivland or Tiv nation, *Tar Tiv*, is a sweeping reference to the Tiv people of Nigeria. The Tiv are domiciled in Benue, Nassarawa, Taraba, Plateau, Niger, and the Federal Capital. They are also found in significant numbers in Southwestern Nigeria, where they form part of the farming communities in Ekiti, Osun, Ogun, and Oyo states. Wherever they are found, their principal occupation is farming. The present Population of the Nigerian Tiv is 11,000,000 people, constituting 5% of Nigeria's 211,366,891 million people. By 2050, the Tiv population is expected to rise to over 15,000,000 million.[2]

The Protestants' and Catholics' encounter with the Tiv was after the establishment of the Northern protectorate in 1900 under the High Commissioner Lord Frederick Lugard. The entire Tiv country was unaware that they had been included in the massive colonial enterprise and had been colonised. They were neither part

---

1 Professor Iyorwuese Hagher, an accomplished academic, diplomat, and politician, is President, African Leadership Institute, USA.

2 See https://www.macrotrends.net also https://www.worldmeter.info-ng.

of the negotiated sale of land as claimed by the colonialists nor had suffered any defeat at war from the British, Fulani, or any other warring entities. The career of Lord Lugard who later amalgamated Nigeria, significantly changed the course of Tiv history and other minority tribes of the Middle Belt of Nigeria.

Lugard and his wife Flora Shaw believed that the Fulani who had a fairer skin and claimed kinship with Arabs were more intelligent and more skilled in administration than the darker-skinned inhabitants of the Middle-Belt and the Southern parts of Nigeria. He proudly and famously founded the Indirect Rule policy that authorised the Sokoto Caliphate to sub-colonise other tribes in the Northern Protectorate and Islamise and *Hausafy* them through Islam, the sharia law, the Hausa language, costumes, and culture. He permitted the establishment of Evangelical Churches in the Middle Belt, but stoutly prevented the sphere of the Sokoto Caliphate from the influence of Christianity. He protected the Caliphate's Muslim religion and their system of governance that was constructed on conquest.[3]

The Roman Catholics in Nigeria

The entry of the Roman Catholics in Nigeria predated colonialism. As far back as 1487, the Portuguese Roman Catholic Mission in the Benin Empire (now mostly Edo State) thrived.[4] But this Catholic Mission fizzled out as the Portuguese lost sea power supremacy and the British took over. Britain promoted the Slave trade that boomed for three centuries. It was during this period

[3] For detailed Biography on Lord Frederick Lugard. See Rory O'Grady, *The Passionate Imperialist: The True Story of Sir Frederick Lugard and Flora Shaw* (The Conrad Press, the United Kingdom, 2018).

[4] See www.thehistoryville.com/christianity-abenkulaE.N.

that the Protestant Reformation took place. With the abolition of the slave trade and the birthing of colonialism, interest in bringing Christianity to the colonies assumed currency. This interest was in the form of various Christian expeditions led by inter-denominational Protestant Churches and missionary societies rather than the Roman Catholics.

The Missionary Societies and Explorers

Abeokuta is recorded as having the first missionary station in Nigeria in 1843. The pioneering work of Birch Freedman, Rev. Henry Townsend, and Samuel Ajayi Crowther in setting up this mission is very well documented.[5] It was a decade later in 1854 that the first contact was made with the Tiv by a British naval officer Dr W. B. Baike. This unfortunate contact set the tone for the denigration of the Tiv in official colonial records and beyond, that the Tiv were a peculiar tribe of lawless cannibals and total barbarians. Unlike other tribes, the Tiv had resisted the intrusion of strange white people conducting affairs on their land without their permission. Their facial scarification marks were meant for beautification and form of identification, and not meant to give offense to the British Naval Officer Baike, who lacked understanding of this identity. Armed with Baike's unfortunate Tiv stereotype, Lord Lugard, the Governor-General in the gleeful aftermath of his conquest of the Sokoto Caliphate 1903 and the Borno Empire 1904, moved against the Tiv to wage war and punish them for killing some British Officers in Abinsi. It was at this stage that he was recalled back to England, in 1906.

---

5 Ibid.

First Entry of the Gospel in Tivland

The entry of the gospel to Tivland was indeed through Dr Herman Karl Wilhelm Kumm, a German, who pioneered the Sudan United Mission (SUM) in Northern Nigeria.[6] At its very inception, the Sudan United Mission was conceived as inter-denominational, and its sole and urgent task was to counteract the spread of Islam among the indigenous black Africans South of the Sahara. In 1904 Dr Kumm led the expedition that made the first contact with the Tiv at Abinsi. His desire was to plant the South African branch of the SUM in Tivland at Udei, the most westerly part of Tivland. The American branch of the SUM had started work with the Jukun and looked at the adjoining Tivland as their expansion field so was not happy with this. Dr Kumm then directed the South African SUM to divert to the Dili hills and start work with the Mbula tribe. This did not work out because the adjoining Muslim community felt affronted by the idea of a separate religion being introduced by the white missionaries in their sub-colonial space.

The Tiv population became a deciding factor when, at the First Intermission Conference of the evangelical Churches working in Northern Nigeria, a decision was taken that it would be more rewarding for them to evangelise the bigger tribes with populations of 50,000 and above. The Tiv population then was over 200,000 compared to the Mbula with 8,000, Bachama with 19,000, and Tangali with 37,000. The missionaries were enticed with rich farmlands to be exploited apart from the message of the gospel.[7]

On 17th April 1911, the gospel of Christ reached Tivland at the eastern Tiv village of Saaiutu Deekpe, in the Shitile clan. The

---

6 Benjamin Shii, *Christianity in Tivland, A History of the NKST* (Oracle Business Limited, 2011), 54.

7 Casalegg 10, "The land will yield its fruit." Unpublished Manuscript, 95a.

bearer of the gospel was through the Dutch Reformed Church Mission branch of the Sudan United Mission in South Africa. The first evangelist was Dr Karl Zimmerman. This first step for Christianity has blossomed today in many churches, missions, pastors, fathers, and bishops.

The First Encounter

It is difficult for us to cast our mind back to the first encounter between the white missionaries and the Tiv when they attempted to introduce the Christian gospel. In Tivland like most of the Middle Belt, the tribes accommodated the Christian missionaries and the message of Christ, while in further Northern Nigeria, Christianity received nothing but coldness and hostility. It was this same spirit of accommodation and hospitality that the indigenous tribes of the middle-belt welcomed the Muslims and Christians. Today the religions of Islam and Christianity have waged bitter wars in the Middle Belt, contesting for influence and dominance.

In matters of faith and knowledge of God, the Protestants and Catholics that first encountered the Tiv may have also seen them as the most primitive and savage humanity as was peddled and touted by Baikie, the missionary societies, and early ethnographers. But these explorers, ethnographers, and early missionaries were wrong. The Tiv had a strong knowledge of the mighty God who intervened in their affairs continually. They knew the God who in his anger sent thunder, and axes, and lighting. They knew he was very near to the earth but went further in the sky after a woman, had in pounding yams with her pestle, touched God in the groin, and so God gave man space on earth and retreated further into the sky. They knew that the gerontocratic elders communicated with God, and would call on God during times of wars and distress and set out various rituals to repair their land and the priesthood of religious men who were set apart to administer these rituals to bring physical and spiritual healing in Tiv Country.

No wonder, when the white Dutch Reformed Church Mission (DRCM) first encountered the Tiv elders at Saaitu, in the Shitile clan, and told them they wanted to teach them about God, their reaction was not of innocence or childish glee. Contrary to the assumption of the white missionaries, the Tiv mind was not a naive *Tabula Rasa*. The NKST historian, Benjamin Ityavkase Shie, describes this encounter succinctly: *When the elders met at the request of Tor Saaitu Deekpe, in his compound, the missionaries told the people that they would like to settle among them and talk to them about God. The Tiv were bewildered and asked, 'What has God done?'*[8]

The question, *what has God done?* is an explosive meta-narrative of the counter-intuitive consciousness. The Tiv did not wait for the white man to teach him about God. He knew that he was in charge of the land, and the elders had authority and were both historically, and demographically in charge of all things pertaining to the regulation of God's manifestations in the land. They wanted to know the very nature of the white man's complaint about God's latest manifestation. *What has God done.... lately?* The elders in asking this question knew that whatever God had done now was consequential and grievous enough to bring the white man who was apparently running away from God's caprice to report at the Tiv gerontocratic court for a quick solution, and reparation.

The Tiv gerontocrats had in the past called on their God to bring down the rain during drought periods, and invoked his power in fertility rites and stood like Job in the Biblical times to profess their righteousness in times of deep distress to invoke God and dared to plead their innocence and declare that: *Ibyo sen ishô kondô*, Translated; Let guilt descend and righteousness arise. The core existential challenge of Protestants and Catholics in Tivland

---

[8] Shii, *Christianity in Tivland,* 54.

is to answer the question. What has God done? What has he done in the last hundred years of Catholicism in Tivland? The entire missionary effort has been to show the Tiv what God had done and is still doing among the Tiv, that they were not as yet aware of. The story of God's salvation to mankind through the redemptive power of God's son has been the message of both the Catholics and Protestants in Tivland. The evidence of what God had done and has been doing is the testimony of many like me today who, but for the grace of God, would never have had a western education nor received Christ as our personal saviour. The thousands of Tiv graduates today, and hundreds of Tiv clergy that took over from the white Protestant and Catholic missionaries are all the answer to what God had done, has done, and is doing in our midst.

The missionaries and colonialists veiled the encounter between the white missionaries and the Tiv in cognitive dissonance that was exploited. According to Benjamin Shii, when the white missionaries asked for permission to settle and talk to them about God and the hosts were persuaded that God had not done anything grievous that required Tiv gerontocratic intercession: *The people wondered if the missionaries meant to herald God's coming. It surprised the Tiv to no end but they accepted the request.*[9]

The dissonance was, the white missionaries and colonialists allowed themselves to be portrayed as representatives of God, which they were in a way of speaking, spiritually. But the Tiv expected the physical presence of God after the herald had come to prepare the ground for his arrival. The Missionaries and colonialists basked in this dissimulation to the extent that the Tiv now enthroned God as the King and the White man as his deputy. Hence the saying: *Aôndô ka Tor Buter ka Alkali.*

---

9 Ibid.

The missionaries subsequently joined the colonialists to criminalise Tiv culture in polygamy, exchange marriage, and the possession of ritual emblems. The encounter was not smooth and after twenty years, the encountered station at Saaitu was not just shut down, the station was burnt down by the DRCM missionaries as unproductive.

Roman Catholics in Tivland: Conflicts and Cooperation with the NKST[10]

When one looks at the immense work done by the Catholic Church today in health, education, and social justice alongside the NKST Church in Tivland, one can really appreciate the grace of God for the harmony existing between the Protestants and Catholics in Tivland. In the Tiv context today in the same eastern side of Tiv where the gospel first arrived, Catholic priests and NKST pastors are being killed by rampaging Tiv youth bandits and their Fulani guest terrorists. A nightmare is unfolding before our eyes of a post-Christian Tivland where the youth have abandoned the Christian faith and the God of their fathers. They have regressed and are busy worshipping the Fulani-made amulets and gris-gris, while they kill, maim and rape with horrendous impunity.

The NKST and the Catholic, have both come a long way to bring God to the Tiv through the use of the same Bible translated mainly by the NKST, as well as the use of the traditional music of the Tiv, with deeply meaningful spiritual songs. The universal Catholic Church is growing and flourishing with profound fecundity in Tiv country in the worship of the one true God by both Catholics and the NKST. This is the import of what Pope Francis

---

[10] *Nongo u Kristu Ken Sudan hen Tiv* (NKST), literally, "the followers of Christ in the Sudan among the Tiv," Rubingh, *Sons of Tiv*, 89.

said: *I believe in God-not a Catholic God; there is no Catholic God. There is God, and I believe in Jesus Christ, his incarnation. Jesus is my teacher and pastor, but God the Father Abba is the light and creator.*[11] In the beginning, it was not so. The European Clergy that introduced Christianity to the Middle Belt and Tivland were greedy to acquire territory. Just like the scramble to colonise, the scramble to missionise became a real battle to acquire territory and adherents. In Europe, after the reformation, and the rebellion of the Church of England, the Catholic faith was often viewed with hostility. This hostility was in existence when the Roman Catholics who were Germans and Irish met the South African white missionaries, in Tiv land.

The DRCM was at pains to ignore the fact that Catholics and Protestants were both a reformation of the Jewish faith following the teachings of Christ. Nor did the DRCM point to the fact that the Apostle's creed of the Protestants and Catholics was an attestation to the belief in the One supreme triune God the Father, Son, and Holy Spirit.

Instead of preaching unity, the DRCM emphasised the different views of Catholics and Protestants in the meaning and authority of the Bible. The DRCM belittled the Catholic belief that God had revealed himself and his plan of salvation from the words of the Bible and from the oral tradition. The DRCM stood strongly against the oral tradition, the basis of the Martin Luther reformation, and relied on the principle of the scripture only, *Sola Scriptura*.

But much more was at stake. The Catholic's met an already conscious Tiv population hungry for new knowledge of God and were better organised to spread the message because of their unitary command structure of one Apostolic Church throughout the

[11] Ones.thefamouspeople.com/popefrancis-4362php.

world, under the leadership of the Pope, who traced his position to the appointment of Peter by Jesus as the first head of the Church. The protestant Churches were already divided in the field. The scramble for territory by the American SUM initially prevented the DRCM SUM from settling in Tiv Country, because they had first settled in the Jukun territory, which was adjoining Tivland, and saw Tivland as their next field for expansion. But later when the American SUM took over the entire Tiv field from the DRCM, their counterparts in Wukari Federation where the Tiv tribe was the largest tribe; instigated the cry for the Tiv in Wukari to be expelled from the Wukari Federation.

The head start of the DRCM of nine years in bringing the gospel to Tivland was challenged by the arrival of the Catholics in 1920 when it seemed the Catholics were trail-brazing across Tivland from their base in the Tiv West while the DRCM was fixated in the Tiv East in Saaitu and Zaki-Biam area. At first, the German Catholic missionaries arrived and concentrated in the hinterland. Then the Irish arrived and moved to the towns. It was due to the arrival of the Catholic Church and their spread across Tivland that the DRCM closed down their first Tiv field in Saaitu as unproductive. In their anger with the people of Saaitu, the DRCM missionaries burnt down the Church building. In the words of Shie, *the Church building was demolished ostensibly to protect it from being misused by Hausa traders.*

Just as the station at Saaitu was closed down, another was raised and the missionaries moved to Jato Aka. The DRCM now spread in rapid sequence to the largest field in Kunav. The main reason was, according to Shie: *it was envisaged that the presence of the Roman Catholics in the area could be better checked.* [12] The

[12] Shii, *Christianity in Tivland,* 81.

encounter between the Catholics and the DRCM quickly turned into a competition for proselytisation. In Kunav area where the DRCM had rushed to build its largest Church, they complained that, *instead of the RCM looking for children who were not in school, they enticed those who were in DRCM schools.* [13]

But the success of the RCM to entice followers of the DRCM into their fold was not just among the school children. DRCM teachers were also offered higher salaries in the RCM. Other enticements were the introduction of the English language teaching and the wholesale entertainment spectacle of Catholic Church rituals and bazaars that endeared the Tiv to the Catholic Church. Furthermore, the DRCM had unwittingly or wittingly unfurled the racism of the DRCM on the native Tiv population. Their unwillingness to teach Tiv in the English language was a calculated attempt to deny them a global education so as to teach them to read and write in their vernacular, and so limit them how to worship God and serve the DRCM. When the first Tiv man to learn the Tiv alphabet in the Dutch orthography, Akiga Sai, penned his letter of gratitude to the DRCM they were ecstatic. The students of the Roman Catholic schools on the other hand were communicating in the English language.

I grew up under the DRCM tutelage, my father was mentored, by Mr Loedorf, the man in charge of the physical structures of the Church. Apart from my father being trained at the Teachers College Mkar as a Vernacular teacher, (VTA and VTB), he learned how to build, sew, and tend to orchards. This knowledge he put to great use when he was entrusted with the responsibility of planting the Gbagir branch of the Church, and opening the primary school. But the DRCM pastors segregated themselves from the congre-

---

13 Shii, *Christianity in Tivland*, 183.

gation. Inside the churches, they sat in segregated pews and also separated the women from the men. This was not all. To become a baptised adult member of the Church took several years. One could take as much as four or five years to be in the seekers' class to qualify for baptism. One of the most important tests to be administered before baptism was proficiency in the Heidelberg Catechism a reformed confession from 1563 with its 129 questions and answers. This permanently branded Catholicism as a Christian sect of doubtful practices and to be shunned at all costs to avoid contagion, by the baptised protestant.

And after baptism, it was quite easy to be disciplined for one or two years, if suspected of infringing the law. This meant the loss of participation in Communion and loss of job wages to mortify their flesh. So the DRCM and the NKST lost trained teachers to the Roman Catholics who paid better wages and were not as strict with the rigid oversight of the personal lives of their congregation.

On doctrinal matters the DRCM/NKST Church were severe. They presented the congregation with a well printed and bound selection of Bible passages called, *Akaa a Bibilo*, or Things about the Bible. Inside these things of the Bible was the prominent story of Noah. The Tiv and all black people were the offending Ham race that was cursed by God and had to accept servility and acquiescence to their righteous superior white race. The congregants competed with each other to show subservience and abjectness as pre-conditions of acceptance as good church members and deserving of heaven in after life.

In 1957 the indigenous NKST took over from the DRCM and in 1960 the DRCM responded to the Nigerian Government's ban on Apartheid and their mission in Tivland. They handed over to the NKST and the American SUM who were more liberal and who planted many churches and expanded on education and health. The encounter of the indigenous NKST Church and the Roman Catholics in Tivland has been one of co-operation and harmony. The biggest harmony has been the introduction of the Tiv Catholics to the Tiv Bible translated by the Bible Societies and the NKST. This giant step for Christianity has been possible by growing liberalisation in the Catholic Church which had hitherto been bound by the Magisterium and Civil authorities stretching as far back as the 16th Century when King Ferdinand and Queen Isabella of Spain made a law prohibiting the possession of any Biblical version, during the time of Pope Paul IV in 1559.

When the NKST and DRCM were writing the Tiv Bible in the 1950's the Roman Catholics in Tivland were bound by the 1950 Encyclical of Pope Pius XII, whose Humani Generis warned *against some dangerous aspect of the new enthusiasm for bible reading* which the Pope was afraid would endanger the *The Truth of the faith and catholic Doctrine.* Happily for all Christians, Pope John Paul of 1959 and Pope Paul 1963 restated the need of all Christians to access the Bible and even added a concession for Catholics to use Bible *translations produced in co-operation with the separated brethren as well.*[14] The only regret the Catholics have in the use of the Tiv Bible is expressed through Rev. Terwase Akaaibiam; *Regrettable the Tiv Bible extensively used by Catholics in Tivland was translated by the Bible Society of Nigeria long ago through interpreters with avoidable mistakes and without the Deutero-canonical books.* [15]

The NKST and the Catholic Church in Tivland are partners to the growth of the Universal Church of Christ in Tiv land. The introduction of Tiv music and song through the promotion of

[14] Terwase H. Akaaibiam. "The Bible in the Catholic Church in Tivland." in *Reflections on the year of faith* (Makurdi: Catholic Dioceses of Makurdi, Gboko and Katsina-Ala, 2013), 57.

[15] Edwin H. Robertson. *Taking the word to the world. 50 years of the United Bible Societies* (Nashville Tennessee, Thomas Nelson Inc., 1996), 108-109.

the legendary Tyavger Fate, the lame NKST singer from Ukan, has now blossomed to every aspect of Tiv worship in the Roman Catholic and NKST Churches. The women have turned out to dominate this peculiar Tiv worship by giving their bodies, hearts and soul; singing and dancing with joy to their one triune God.

The late Bishop Athanasius Usuh's role, in domesticating Catholic worship to Tiv songs and music was profound, and needs to be more acknowledged by mission scholars. The two churches have co-operated on issues of political and social reforms in Tivland, and have worked with the government and traditional institutions on ending banditry and reform of burial rites, marriage rites, and conduct of politics. Both churches have focused on the education and health of the members and the need for a kinder, gentler, and far more community-oriented political leadership. In their pastoral letter, on the eve of the 2015 elections, the Catholic Bishops in Benue State warned against the polity where: *We do not seem to be guided by truth and honesty, love and unity, peace and justice, integrity and uprightness. Forever, God does not seem to play a central role in our daily life.* [16]

In the foreseeable future, we need to see greater cooperation between the two churches and other Christian sects as the national crises deepens amidst the challenges of insurgency, and the Islamisation scare. The rise of uneducated youth in Tivland, in Benue East and in Taraba States, poses an existential challenge to the churches and to Christianity. Like the Catholic Bishops, the President of the NKST, Rev. D. Z. Anza's call on Christian leaders to embrace the attributes of true Christian leadership in 1 Timo-

[16] Statement in the joint Pastoral letter of the Catholic Bishops on the Benue Elections on Benue State 2015, Published by the Catholic Bishops of the Benue State, 2015.

thy 3:4; *Goodness, faithfulness, self-control, respect, helpfulness, gentleness, peacefulness and not be lovers of money,*[17]is poignant.

The world looks on as the NKST and Catholics, together, join hands to confront the existential challenges of humanity in Tivland in the 21st century.

[17] Rev. Dominic Z. Anza. President of the NKST in his inaugural speech of the Benue State Government Cabinet, on 17th September at Benue People's House, Makurdi.

Chapter Two

Advent and Evolution of the Catholic Church in Tivland

Shagbaor F. Wegh[1]

Introduction

In 1868, the Society of African Mission (SMA), led by Francesco Borghero, arrived Lagos, and evangelisation of the area, covered then by the provinces of Lagos, Benin, Ibadan, Jos, and Kaduna, was initiated. The Vicariate Apostolic of the Bight of Benin was created in 1883. The Vicariate Apostolic of the Upper Niger was created in 1884, with its center first in Lokoja and later in Asaba, under the very popular Fr Carlo Zappa.

As happened with the Protestant Mission, the move to the north was halted by British order. However, in 1907 the intrepid Zappa made the 300-mile leap from Asaba to establish the only Catholic station in the north up to the 1930s in Shendam. Westwards, historic Benin, administered from Sapele, got its bishop in 1929 (Thomas Broderick), who was resident in Asaba and moved to Benin in 1939. Issele-Uku Diocese was created in 1973 to take

---

1 Professor Shagbaor F. Wegh, a Catholic priest of Makurdi Diocese is of the Benue State University.

care of the West-Niger Igbo. These were the initial steps that later led to the formation of the three ecclesiastical provinces of Lagos, Ibadan, and Benin.

If Zappa preferred raising Christian communities and did not emphasize education, though he was compelled to do so later, the school in the service of evangelisation became the trademark of the Holy Ghost Fathers [Spiritans], who arrived in Onitsha in December 1885 led by Fr Lutz. The Apostolic Prefecture of the Lower Niger was created in 1889. Fr Leon Lejeune was the architect of the school for evangelisation, and the indefatigable Bishop Joseph Shanahan carried this to its ultimate conclusion leading to massive conversions among the Igbo to Catholicism. The initial evangelisation in the Lower Niger consisted of buying back slaves, instruction to create a Christian community, and healthcare. Lutz and, later, the Sisters of Cluny were noted for their efforts in healthcare.

When Shanahan took over from Lejeune as Prefect in 1905, he capitalised on the Igbo love for education and his own knowledge of their religion to evangelise. "If we go from town to town talking about God, we know from experience that much of our efforts bring no result. But no one is opposed to schools." This sole focus on schools, even to the point of excluding the building of churches, drove a wedge between the original preoccupation of French Spiritans to build Christian communities and the new drive to make converts through the schools. The matter became apparent during the school take-over in 1970.

In his great trek inland, Shanahan established schools and saw the need for more agents of evangelisation. St Patrick's Society (Kiltegan) was founded in 1932 for this particular Mission. The Prefecture of Calabar was created in 1934. As from 1930, Shanahan turned his attention to expand towards the north resulting in the

Prefecture of the Benue (present-day Makurdi, Gboko and Katsina Ala Dioceses).[2]

In 1986 Fr Hassen relived his experience:

> Conditions were difficult in the 1930s, but not in the same sense that we have them today. Today, the leading cause of hardship is the devaluation of the naira, the country's official currency, which has been brought about by the government's futile attempt to reconstruct the economy without first constructing an economic base. It is like climbing a tree from the top!! Thus, the goods are there, but the naira is so valueless that only a few individuals can afford to have enough to purchase even the basic goods. Another area is the communication and transportation system. The country's communication network and transportation system are excellent compared to what was obtainable in the 1930s. There were no roads, no motor cars, and the railway did not pass through most of the areas these missionaries were to cover.
>
> Every missionary journey was done on foot. They used to trek, day and night, bringing the good news at the doorsteps of the villagers, who had the option, either to accept or reject the new faith. As mentioned earlier, there were numerous disadvantages. The harsh climate, the mosquitoes, the snakes and other harmful insects whose contact with the missionaries kept them in bed for weeks. Thus missionary activities in these areas Christianity were erratic and moved at a slow pace. "There was an atmosphere of peace wherever we went," said Fr Hassen "The men would gather and listen to our message through an interpreter. After this they would disperse, some to their farms, and others to hunting. But they allowed their children to attend our Sunday Schools. Here we taught them how to sing, to read and write. The people put up no organised resistance to our messages.[3]

---

2 Catholic Secretariat of Nigeria: *Church in Nigeria: Family of God on Mission Lineamenta for the First National Pastoral Congress* (Abuja: Catholic Secretariat of Nigeria, 2012).

3 Mato Clement, "The Catholic Church in Tivland" in *Catholic Diocese of Makurdi at 50: A Celebration of Service to Humanity*. Edited by Shagbaor F. Wegh (Makurdi:

The ecclesiastical territories today called the Dioceses of Makurdi, Gboko, and Katsina Ala were part of the newly formed Prefecture Apostolic of the lower Niger between 1889 and 1920. The Prefecture covered the entire land area east of the River Niger and the South of River Benue. In 1920 its status within the Catholic Church was raised to that of Vicariate Apostolic of Southern Nigeria though maintaining its boundaries.

The missionary priests who first evangelised in this area were French Holy Ghost Fathers. They were joined by Holy Ghost Priests and brothers from Ireland, and it was the latter who from 1911 began to make contact with the Benue in the Northern part of the Vicariate.

The Tiv of the Middle-Belt

Since this write-up deals with the Catholic Church in Tivland it is not out of place to say something brief about the Tiv who are actually the target here. Tivland is located in Benue State, one of the Thirty-six states of Nigeria's present political structure. Benue State is situated in the middle of the country, and therefore is within the geographical area known as the Middle-Belt. The Tiv, who are the most populous ethnic group in the Middle-Belt with an estimated population of over seven million, are also referred to in literature and popularly as the Tiv of the Middle-Belt.

The Tiv are no strangers to both Western and African writers. Western literary accounts do not hide the fascination of Westerners with them. They have been regarded as enigmatic people. Western literature is also full of controversy regarding Tiv character. Bohannan has remarked that the Tiv are of an independent turn of mind and are almost indeed one of the most ethnocentric

Selfers Academic Press Ltd, 2010), 40-45.

peoples in the world. Bohannan, quoting Frobenius, says "they are the most practical and unsuperstitious people I have found in Africa." Lugard, the British High Commissioner Tiv, after several unsuccessful campaigns against them, listed them amongst those extremely truculent tribes among whom it was not safe to travel. Downes affirms that the Tiv had resisted the Muslims, the Hausa, and Fulani who pressed down from the north and were little affected by the Ibo and other Nigerian tribes of the south. Downes submits that the Tiv were one of the last tribes in Nigeria to be brought under the rule imposed by the Colonial government.[4]

A hundred years ago, none of the early missionaries who started the work of evangelisation in Tivland would have imagined the phenomenal growth of the Church in this part of the world. It is feasible that we begin this write-up with a bird's eye view of the beginning of the Catholic Church in Nigeria. The Tiv believe that they are all children of a man called Tiv. Tiv had two sons – *Ichongu* (circumcised) and *Ipusu* (uncircumcised). All Tiv believe that they are one in the person of their ancestor Tiv and draw their identity and a sense of solidarity from him. Following that, the individual sees himself/herself as continuous with the community.

Before the coming of the British colonial administration, they practiced *Yamishe* (exchange marriage). That is the marriage system by the exchange of *angor (sisters/daughters)* between individuals; the exchanged sisters become wives. Exchange marriage was anchored on the ideology of the continuity of the family or lineage. It was the primary form of marriage.

The colonial administration abolished exchange marriage in 1927. The price which the Tiv had to pay was high. Exchange marriage had been a powerful deterrent against social disintegra-

4 Downes R.M, *Tiv Religion* (Ibadan: Ibadan University Press, 1971), Vii.

tion since it created mutual dependencies and responsibilities. The abolition meant that the totality of the Tiv world view symbolised and expressed in exchange marriage was shattered.

The Tiv have a great love for the family. The term used to express the notion of family is *tsombur* (umbilical cord). The umbilical cord is the tube that connects the unborn child to the mother. Through that, the unborn get nourishment. Used metaphorically, *tsombur* implies that family members are joined together in a sort of organic union. This is good for the support and sustenance of family members. The Tiv cherish children and large families. The greatest outcome of marriage is children, who are a sign of prosperity and bestow prestige on their parents. Through children, the Tiv see a long prosperous future before them. The deep sense of solidarity traced back to Tiv; the progenitor imposes the duty to continue the family through offspring. [5]

Pope Benedict XV and the Tiv Mission

The strategy to evangelise the Lower Benue was hinged on the notion of the "Tiv Mission." The idea was to launch an evangelising drive from Ogoja in Cross River State. Tivland was part of the former Apostolic Prefecture of the Lower Niger. Fr Alexander Leon Lejeune, C.S.S.P., who succeeded Fr Rene Pawlas, C.S.S.P., as Apostolic Prefect is believed to be the first to make contacts with the Tiv people.[6] After the death of Fr Lejeune in 1905, Propaganda Fide appointed Pere Douvry Apostolic Administrator for Cameroon in February 1917, a daunting task which he carried out commendably well. Douvry was always anxious to return

5 Cf. Shagbaor F. Wegh. *Between Continuity and Change: Tiv Concept of Tradition and Modernity* (Enugu: SNAAP Press Ltd, 2003).

6 Catholic Diocese of Gboko, 2021 Diary & Directory, 21.

to Nigeria to carry out a project that seems to have haunted him for many years, to bring the Gospel to the Tiv people. The initial plan was to open a new mission at Ogoja, outside Igboland, to spring into Tiv country. In March 1921 Douvry spent two months traveling among the Tiv. He met the Chiefs of Katsina-Ala division and three-quarters of those of Abinsi. Everywhere he went, he was well received, and the people promised to send their children to school. Unfortunately, Douvry had to withdraw from Ogoja because of ill-health. He subsequently returned to France and died in 1924.

On June 6, 1920, Fr Joseph Shanahan, C.S.S.P., was appointed Bishop and made Vicar Apostolic of the New Vicariate of Southern Nigeria. He sent priests to Calabar and Ogoja, who reached out to places like Obudu, Ikom, Kakwagom, and Tivland. When Bishop Shanahan visited Pope Benedict XV in September 1920, he took Douvry along and presented him to the Pope. In an excited letter written to Mgr. LeRoy, from the French Seminary, Shanahan submitted:

> Today I had the great joy and honour of being received by His Holiness Benedict XV in private audience. He asked me many questions about the Mission of the Southern Nigeria. I asked His Holiness the favour of presenting to him Pere Douvry who is going to found a new station amongst a tribe which numbers millions of people. Pere Douvry entered and on his knees, asked amongst other things for a special blessing[5]. The Holy Father Blessed both Pere Douvry and the new Mission to the (Tiv).[7]

Fr Douvry's successor at Ogoja was Fr Eugene Goetz. Fr Goetz soon realised the weakness of trying to approach the Tiv from Ogoja. The weakness lay in the fact that Ogoja, from where

---

[7] (Arch. Gen. 192B VIII).

he was expected to conduct the Tiv mission was far from Tivland. He further pointed out that the Tiv spoke the same language, unlike the Ogoja situation where fifteen different languages were spoken, making evangelisation painfully slow. Furthermore, the Tiv had a powerful antipathy for anything coming from southern Nigeria, which would not augur well for a mission launched from Ogoja. Goetz submitted that the Tiv were wary of any newcomer, so it would be no use making a rare and rapid appearance amongst them if they wished to gain their confidence. Goetz thought that to get to the Tiv, one would have to live amongst them and learn their language.

The Tiv Mission project that had generated so much enthusiasm was, however, dropped. This may have confirmed Fr Groetz's fears that it was not feasible to carry out the project from Ogoja. Whatever the reason for the project's cancellation, it remains instructive that Ogoja Mission seems to have lost its Tiv orientation, and a letter from Shanahan to the Superior General in 1924 talks of a month's visit to Ogoja Mission without any mention of the Tiv entirely.

In 1929, Fr Joseph Soul, one of the General Councillors, came to the Vicariate for an official visitation. At the end of his visit, he had time to spare, so he visited Obudu and, from there, moved into Tivland. Soul spent a short time among the Tiv, but the impressions did not leave him when he returned to Paris. He kept thinking about the abandoned state of the Tiv and all other people of Northern Nigeria.

Fr Soul's visit to Tivland was, however, providential. The accidental visit resulted in the Spiritans finally deciding to make some serious attempt to evangelise the people of the Lower Benue, the Tiv, Idoma, Igala, and other smaller groups. German Spiritans took up the task, and by 1930 the first contingent of four priests and two brothers arrived, precisely 45 years after Joseph Lutz and his companies established themselves at Onitsha. Their Apostolic zeal and energy were such that by 1934 the areas of the civil territory of Benue province, Northern Nigeria, was made into the Prefecture Apostolic of Benue Province with its center first at Makurdi, and later at Otukpo.

The First Missionaries to Arrive in Makurdi

The first group of missionaries arrived in Makurdi by train. It was on the 30th October 1930. The team was made up of four missionaries, namely, two priests Winterle and Kirsten, and two Brothers Maurice and Remigius. With the team's arrival, the only existing Catholic Church building at Makurdi, namely the Resthouse and the Catechist's house, became their only dwelling places. The priests moved into the rest house while the brothers occupied the Catechist's house. Catechist Christopher Obi was displaced. The German priests and brothers made tremendous efforts and covered the whole area from Idah on the River Niger to Wukari near Benue and Adamawa provinces. A significant setback came after the outbreak of the Second World War in 1939, as all the priests and brothers being German nationals, were constrained by British authorities to leave Nigeria. By 1945 when those from the English province replaced the German fathers, Bishop Heery described the Benue as the most promising Mission in all of Nigeria after Onitsha-Owerri.

From the Old Catholic Diocese of Makurdi to the Present Dioceses.

When Makurdi Diocese was established, all of Tivland was under it, and since the Diocese became the powerhouse of Tiv evangelisation, we need to look at the emergence of the diocese itself. In 1959 Monsignor James Hagan, the Prefect Apostolic of Otukpo, and was made Bishop of Makurdi, thus becoming the first Bishop of Makurdi in 1960. The Tiv Mission project had metamorphosed into the Catholic Diocese of Makurdi. Ill-health, however, forced him to resign in 1966. This led to the emergence in January 1968 of Bishop Murray as the second Bishop of Makurdi.

For the 21 years that Bishop Murray administered the Diocese, the Church experienced phenomenal growth in various aspects of ecclesiastical life. The prophecy of Bishop Heery was fulfilled as the Diocese became one of the fastest-growing dioceses in Nigeria and, arguably, Africa.

The hope of a genuinely indigenous Church became fully realised when, on 21st October 1989, Most Rev Athanasius Atule Usuh became the Bishop of Makurdi, following the retirement of Bishop Murray. Under Bishop Usuh, Makurdi Diocese continued to experience tremendous growth. This was evident in the creation of the Dioceses of Otukpo in 1995 and Lafia in 2001, respectively. Then in 2012, Bishop Usuh achieved the feat of creating two dioceses, Gboko and Katsina/Ala, in one fell swoop. At the creation of Gboko and Katsina/Ala Dioceses, Makurdi Diocese had a Catholic population of 1,558,638, 210 Diocesan priests, 54 parishes, and 212 major seminarians. The table below shows the growth that is taking place in the Tiv Catholic Church.

Current Statistical Information on Tiv Catholic Dioceses

	Priests	Parishes	Quasi-Parishes	Senior Seminarians	Catholic population
Makurdi	62	18	48	91	978, 188
Gboko	248	32	49	80	1, 301, 740
K/ALA	65	32	-	40	444,680

Source: *Makurdi, Gboko, Katsina-Ala Directory and Diaries, 2021*

Conclusion

It is justifiable to conclude a write-up on the advent and evolution of the Catholic Church in Tivland by drawing attention to the attacks being faced by the Church and the people in general.

For more than a decade now, Benue State has been under attacks from Fulani herdsmen. These attacks have been well orchestrated and executed with sophisticated weaponry. The people of the state believe that these attacks aim to run over the indigenous populations, uproot them from their ancestral lands, and confiscate their lands for settlement and grazing of cows. Hundreds of innocent people have been killed or maimed. Thousands have been displaced from their homes and forced to live in Internally Displaced People's Camps, with untold hardship.

In the course of this pogrom the Catholic Church has not been spared. Quite painfully, she lost two of her priests: Frs Joseph Gor and Felix Tyolaha, VC to the attacks. Many parishes have been closed down. Two priests: Frs Bitrus Abege and Dominic Tarkighir, ordained in 2021 for Makurdi, could not say their first mass in their home parish. A similar scenario is playing out in different parts of Tivland. The Tiv Church is therefore facing challenges from enemies of Christianity.

Chapter Three

The Creation of Catholic Dioceses in Tivland

Moses Aondover Iorapuu[1]

Introduction

This chapter undertakes a critical historical analysis of the Catholic Missionary Enterprise in Tivland. The Tiv people are among the largest minority tribes in Nigeria, and occupy the Benue Valley in the Middle Belt region of central Nigeria. They are the largest ethnic group in Benue state and found in large numbers in other states such as Taraba, Nasarawa, Cross River, Oyo, and the Federal Capital Territory, and in the Republic of Cameroon. They are predominantly Christians and one out in three can be assumed to be Catholic, even though there are other denominations such as the NKST, the Anglicans, the Methodists and the Pentecostals. Besides the Ibo people of eastern Nigeria, no other tribe in Nigeria is reputed to be as Catholic as the Tiv.

In spite of this numerical strength, there had been nothing to demonstrate the growth of Catholicism in Tivland, except the existence of one large entity called Makurdi Diocese; hence the creation of two additional dioceses in Tivland became a watershed in

1 Fr Moses Aondover IORAPUU, Ph.D., is the founding editor of the MEd Journal, editor-in-chief Catholic Star Newspaper, and Director of Communications, Catholic Diocese of Makurdi, Nigeria.

the growth of Catholicism among a people whose embrace of the faith was legendary. This chapter takes into account a brief background of the advent of Christianity among the Tiv and their first encounters with a different Christian sect before Catholicism; the point of entry of Catholic Missionaries; the creation of Makurdi Diocese; and the activities that led to the creation of Gboko and Katsina-Ala Dioceses and the impact of these dioceses on Tivland.

Three-pronged Missionary Descent on Tivland

The Tiv nation is made up of the two distinctive families sired by the two sons of Tiv: Ipusu and Ichongo, which produced the number of children known today as clans. The Ipusu has ten local government areas: Vandeikya, Konshisha, Kwande, Ushongo, Katsina-Ala, Gboko, Tarka, Buruku, Logo and Ukum. The Ichongo has four local government areas: Guma, Gwer-East, Gwer-West and Makurdi. However, according to Dzurgba, family, religious, social, economic and political tensions and fears, caused intra-clan, intra-district and inter-district migration among the Tiv leading to the migration of some of Ipusu family members like Ugondo to Ugba in Logo and Turan in Kwande local government areas of Benue State and beyond.[2]

The vastness of Tivland, both in population and landmass, reported then to be over a million and the largest tribe in the Middle Belt, therefore, does not admit of a single entry point for the missionaries. While there is a general assumption of the first contact of the Tiv with the missionaries, records show that there were multiple points of entry taking into account the different clans. Although the Tiv language is homogenous with no distinct dialect

---

2 See Dzurgba Akpenpuum, *On the Tiv of Central Nigeria: A Cultural Perspective*, (Ibadan: John Archers Publishers, 2007), 22-23.

and understood by all,[3] the contact the Tiv people had with the missionaries took place at different points and times. There are discrepancies and some accounts are incoherent due to inadequate historical records among the Tiv themselves, but convergence is found in the similarity of some essential details.

Nigeria's sea coast was the main entry of missionaries, (North Africa and northern Nigeria were already Islamic enclaves) except those who might have used the Cameroon borders with Benue, Adamawa and Taraba states. Eugene Rubingh, one of the most respected ethnographers of the Tiv people wrote that the first known Christian influence in Nigeria came at the hands of Portuguese Roman Catholic Missionaries during the Middle Ages, as they sailed down the coast of Africa in their search for a way to India. Portuguese missionaries were working in Benin in 1487, and in 1504 the Oba of Benin requested that more missionary teachers be sent to his land.[4] Slave trade as an international business was introduced by the Portuguese but with the decline of Portugal as a major sea-power, the Dutch and the English took over.

> In 1562 an Act was passed by the English Parliament legalizing the purchase of negroes. In 1771 no less than 192 slave-ships left England for Africa. However, since the primary adventure was slavery and the climate was hostile to the Europeans, the gospel message was still not proclaimed until 1841 when the Niger Expedition left England to acquire more information on the major languages in this area, tropical diseases, and to make treatise with local chiefs for the abolition of slave trade to prepare grounds for the planting of the gospel. On board the three steamships of the Royal Navy, there were Africans among them, Samuel Ajayi Crowther, who later became

---

3 Ibid.

4 Rubingh Eugene, *Sons of Tiv*. (Michigan: Baker Book House, 1969), 44-45. In 1538 three other missionaries arrived, but by then the Oba was no longer interested and the effort died. When the English entered in the nineteenth century, few traces of their missionary could be found.

> the Bishop of the Niger. Within two months of arrival in August 1841, forty of the 145 Europeans on board were dead...It had been the hope of the Niger Expedition to travel up the Niger River and then up the Benue. Had these hopes been fulfilled, the party would have passed through the domain of a large tribe called the Tiv. It was not until 1854, however, that the outside world would hear of the Tiv people.[5]

The end of slavery therefore facilitated the expansion of missionary activities, as the liberated African slaves like Samuel Ajayi Crowther, became apostles among their people and where the Europeans failed because of the harsh climate, they provided manpower. Worthy of note is the fact that no Catholic has been traced among returnee missionaries who brought the gospel to the Benue Province.

In 1854 there was a new Niger Expedition, led by an officer of the Royal Navy called Dr. W.B. Baikie; following the disastrous earlier expedition. This time around it was a modest attempt with only one ship and a handful of Europeans who had Quinine, the new-found treatment for the deadly malaria. The team traveled up Benue and returned safely. Even then, the Tiv tribe with over a million people was by far the largest tribe in the Middle Belt. "It was on this journey that a European first encountered the Tiv and reported their existence to the outside world (and that in less than glowing terms). They were at that time called Munshi or Mitshis (a Hausa designation resented by the Tiv because of the derogatory

---

5 Rubingh, *Sons of Tiv*. 45-46.

suggestion of cannibalism in the appellation,"[6] and originally administered from Onitsha in the east to Taraku-Makurdi, thanks to the railway, through the coast from Ogoja in the south into Korinya and then from Shendam, Jos diocese to Udei on the north bank side of River Benue.[7]

The Catholic Church flourished in Tivland, overtaking in its growth all the areas surrounding Tivland that had witnessed missionary activities before it. These points of entry symbolise and attest to the historical background of early encounters with the missionaries, and the creation of the following parishes: Sacred Heart Parish Udei from Guma local government area, St Patrick's Parish Taraku in Gwer local government area, St Theresa's Parish Naka in Gwer-West local government area (all in present day Makurdi Diocese); and St Joseph's Parish Korinya in Konshisha local government area, now under Gboko Diocese. Father Douvry for instance, was said to have visited Katsina-Ala from Ogoja but no Catholic Church was established there, the area of Katsina-Ala being already dominated by the Protestants.

Arrival of Early Missionaries in Benue

The first missionaries in this region were not of the Catholic Church but of the Dutch Reformed Church Mission, (DRCM) from South Africa and the Sudan United Mission (SUM), and by

---

6 Ibid, 48-50.

7 Nnubia Christopher, *Vicariate Forane (Deanery) In the Particular Church*, (Lagos: Sovereign Prints Nig. Ltd, 2019), 181-183.

1957 DRCM became fully indigenous as the *Nongo u Kristu Ken Sudan hen Tiv* (NKST).[8] Rubingh describes the arrival of the early missionaries in Tivland graphically:

> The first twenty years comprise a period of putting the seed into inhospitable soil through a determined penetration of all of Tivland. At the time of the original entrance of the DRCM into Saai in 1911, work was confined by government order to the Tiv that might be living east of Saai, and Saai was itself in the eastern edge of Tivland. In 1912, however, the entire area, east of the Katsina-Ala was opened for missionary travel and settlement. A second station was thereupon opened at Zaki-Biam in 1913, and in 1919 at Sevav. In 1923 permission was received for the first station west of the Katsina-Ala River, to be established at Mkar, which would later become the headquarters of the mission.[9]

Many Tiv people today are either NKST or Catholic, and the greater part of human and institutional development of the Tiv na-

---

8 The acronym NKST originally meant and it still means for the rural people, "Nongo u Kristu Ken Sudan hen Tiv," literally, the followers of Christ in the Sudan among the Tiv. The somewhat incongruous presence of the term Sudan in the name is explained by the fact that the Tiv Church is one of a group of eight all of whom are known as The Church of Christ in the Sudan, who are joined in fellowship (in Hausa: Tarrayyar) of Churches in what was formerly the Northern Region of Nigeria. This area is part of the broad sub-Saharan Belt running across Africa, geographically dominated by the Sudan. The ideal embedded in the name is thus that all the evangelical churches of this huge area might be known by one name. It should also be remembered, more immediately, that most of these churches arose through the auspices of the Sudan United Mission, a mission made up of branches from several denominations, and in whose name the same ideal is incorporated, (Rubingh, Sons of Tiv People p.11). The current NKST however stands for the "Nongu u Kristu u i Ser u Sha Tar" means Universal Reformed Christian Church. This is the attempt by the modern leadership of the Church to make the Church that was hitherto tribal and exclusively Tiv more inclusive, embracing other tribes through the use of the English language.

9 Rubingh, *Sons of Tiv*, 122. The first baptism among the Tiv took place on December 30, 1917. Four men were baptised including Akiga Sai the first Tiv man to be educated (p.92). All these accounts depict the presence of Protestants in one part of Tivland, the present-day Katsina-Ala Diocese, which informs the absence of a strong Catholic Church presence here until in the 70s.

tion can only be attributed to these two denominations. Although the church arrived late among the Tiv people, this brief and late encounter transformed into a tremendous and beautiful growth of the church in both the NKST and the Catholic.

The Arrival of the Catholic Church in Tivland

The Dutch Reformed Church Mission and the Sudan United Mission made first entry into Tivland through River Benue up the eastern side of Saai in Katsina-Ala. The Catholic Missionaries were however on their heels, especially with the construction of the rail lines that began from the south to the north of Nigeria. The ecclesiastical territory which is today called Makurdi Diocese was part of the newly formed Prefecture Apostolic of the Lower Niger between 1889 and 1920. The Prefecture covered the entire land area within the east of the River Niger and to the south of River Benue. In 1920, its status within the Catholic Church was raised to that of Vicariate Apostolic of Southern Nigeria, though maintaining its boundaries. In 1880 the first missionary priests, the French Holy Ghost Fathers, began to evangelise in this area. They were joined by Holy Ghost priests and brothers from Ireland; it was the latter that in 1911 began to make contact with the Benue in the northern part of the Vicariate.[10]

The strategy to evangelise the Lower Benue was hinged on the notion of the "Tiv Mission." The idea was to launch an evangelising drive from Ogoja in Cross River State. In February 1917 Propaganda Fide appointed Perė Douvry Apostolic Administrator for the whole of Cameroon; it was a daunting challenge. He returned to Paris in August 1920 and resigned as Apostolic Administrator. Douvry was nevertheless always anxious to return to Nigeria and

[10] Catholic Church in Nigeria, Official Directory (2017-2020), 619.

to bring the gospel to the Tiv people. Documents from Makurdi Diocese show that Joseph Shanahan, the Vicar Apostolic for the Tiv project visited Pope Benedict XV in September 1920 and presented Perė Douvry whom the Holy Father gave special blessing for the Tiv Mission and who had to return to Nigeria. Father Douvry was succeeded by Father Eugene Groetz.[11]

The history of Ogoja Diocese records that on December 5, 1885, Fr Lutz, a Holy Ghost priest from France arrived Onitsha. He died in 1895 and Fr Alexander Lejeune succeeded him. Lejeune was succeeded by Fr Joseph Shanahan, through whose missionary zeal, the Catholic faith reached Calabar, Ogoja, parts of Cross River State, Tivland and the Cameroons. Msgr Shanahan, after his consecration as bishop in 1920 by Pope Benedict XV, requested for a mission in Tivland. The pope granted the request and two priests: Fr Douvry and Fr Mellet were assigned this mission.

When they arrived Ogoja on May 15, 1921 enroute Tivland because of the harsh weather and poor health, they remained temporarily at Ogoja and carried out their work from there to Obudu, Tivland, Wanokom, Kakwagom[12] During this time Douvry visited some places in Tivland, including the chiefs of Katsina-Ala division, Abinsi, a few kilometers from Makurdi and other villages. He was well received among the Tiv, but had to return to France because of ill-health. He died in 1924. He was succeeded by Fr Eugene Groetz, who insisted that for the Tiv Mission to thrive, there was need for one to live permanently among the Tiv and learn their language instead of visiting from Ogoja.

No activity would be reported on a serious scale of the Tiv Mission until in 1929, (but missionary activities were active in places

---

11 Cf. Wegh F. Shagbaor, ed. *Catholic Diocese of Makurdi @ 50: A Celebration of Service to Humanity* (Makurdi: Selfers Academic Press, 2010), 50, 28.

12 Catholic Church in Nigeria, Official Directory (2017-2020), Ogoja Diocese 717.

like Korinya, Taraku, Naka and Makurdi) when Fr Joseph Soul, one of the General Councillors, came to the Vicariate on official visitation. He found time to visit Obudu and entered Tivland and the Tiv people made a lasting impression on him. He kept thinking about the abandoned Tiv Mission until the Spiritans decided on a serious commitment to evangelise the people of the Lower Benue: the Tiv, Idoma, Igala and other smaller tribes.

The church of St Joseph's Korinya was built in 1922, while the Holy Ghost church and school built by the Germans in Makurdi in 1926 are still standing. In the middle of 1930, it was decided that Catholic missionary priests should live on a permanent site in Makurdi. This task was taken up by the German Spiritans.[13] The first group of missionaries to settle in Holy Ghost Parish, Makurdi arrived on October 30, 1930 by train. The team was made up of four missionaries: two priests, Fathers Winterle C.S.Sp. and Kirsten C.S.Sp, and two brothers; Maurice and Remigius. The priests moved into the rest house, while the brothers occupied the Catechist's house.

On November 1, 1930 these missionaries were introduced by Bishop Heerey to the people of Makurdi at a public celebration of the Holy Mass and reception with a huge crowd and the civil authority present. While the missionaries were Germans, the civil authority of Nigeria was under the British. The missionaries quickly began to work on the new church, because the existing one was too small to contain the population at Mass. The construction of the present Holy Ghost Church, which became the first cathedral, began in 1931 and was completed in 1935.[14]

---

13 Wegh, *Catholic Diocese of Makurdi @ 50.* 28-29.

14 Catholic Diocese of Makurdi, Holy Ghost Parish Makurdi Brochure 90th Anniversary 1930-2020.

The Apostolic zeal and energy of the Germans were such that by 1934 the areas of the civil territory of Benue Province, Northern Nigeria was made into the Prefecture Apostolic of Benue with its centre first at Makurdi, and later at Otukpo. The German priests and brothers made fantastic efforts and covered the whole area from Idah on the River Niger to Wukari near the boundary of Benue and Adamawa provinces. A major setback, though, came following the outbreak of World War II in 1939, as all the priests and brothers, being German nationals, were ordered by British authorities to leave Nigeria. There would be a lacuna in missionary activities in Tivland until 1945, when the German Fathers were replaced by the English. Bishop Heerey would describe the Benue as the most promising Mission in all of Nigeria after Onitsha-Owerri. In 1959 Monsignor James Hagan, the Prefect Apostolic of Otukpo, was made a Bishop and in 1960 he transferred his "Cathedral" seat to Makurdi, thus becoming the first Bishop of Makurdi.[15]

The Tiv Mission project had metamorphosed into the Catholic Diocese of Makurdi. However, due to ill-health, Hagan was obliged to resign in 1966. This led to the emergence of Bishop Donal Murray in January 1968 as the second Bishop of Makurdi. Bishop Murray brought phenomenal growth in various aspects of ecclesial life to the diocese. This is evident in the increase in the numbers of religious, diocesan priests, and seminarians and infrastructural growth in education and the health sectors. The first Tiv Catholic priest, the late James Akor, was ordained in 1970 at St John's Church, Gboko.

Bishop Murray was anxious to have an indigenous priest prepared as his successor, and the late Father Thomas Fiery, former secretary to Bishop Hagan and the Cathedral Administrator was

---

15 Nnubia, *Vicariate Forane (Deanery) In the Particular Church,* 186.

asked to prepare Father Akor. James Akor had to start learning the job of becoming the Vicar General as the Cathedral Administrator; so Thomas Fiery had to leave for the United States to raise funds for medical projects in Makurdi diocese through a Foundation known as World Mercy. This Foundation gave birth to the following hospitals in the early 70s: St Mary's Okpoga, now in Otukpo Diocese; St Vincent's Aliade, Makurdi Diocese; and St Thomas' Ihugh, now in Gboko Diocese.[16]

The hope of Bishop Murray for a truly indigenous Church was actualised with the ordination of Father Athanasius Usuh as the coadjutor bishop of the diocese in 1988 and installed on October 21, 1989 following Murray's retirement. Bishop Usuh continued the tremendous vision of Bishop Murray in terms of manpower and general development, evident in the creation of Otukpo Diocese in 1995 and Lafia Diocese in the year 2001.[17]

The Creation of Gboko and Katsina-Ala Dioceses in Tivland

The regions of Gboko and Katsina-Ala that would become dioceses were the two axes the missionaries used in penetrating Tivland: Sai in present day Katsina-Ala Diocese by the Dutch Reformed Church and Mbaduku, Kunav territory right into Korinya, Gaav from Ogoja by the Catholic Church. For instance St Joseph's Church in Korinya, Gaav, was erected in 1920 where the renowned first Catholic secondary school in Tivland, Mount Saint Michael's Secondary School began in 1953 and shortly after, moved to Aliade. St Joseph's Korinya (Korinya) is number

---

16 Moses A. Iorapuu, *The Prophetic Apologist*, (Makurdi: Oracle Business Ltd, 2015), 150.

17 Catholic Church in Nigeria, Official Directory (2017-2020), 500.

twenty-eight among the twenty-nine stations listed in a book of records by the missionaries.[18]

The growth of the Catholic Church in Tivland is astonishingly remarkable considering the fact that only in the early 20th century did the missionaries arrive in this territory. This is better captured in the quote by Rubingh: "According to Father A. C. Edwards of the Roman Catholic Mission in Tivland, the Church does not appear at once full-blown on the scene, but is built up gradually through stages, including in the beginning, semi-pagan or pre-Christian elements. Only in succeeding years does one see the actual Church and the mature Christian believer."[19] Part of this gradual build up could not have been more manifest than among the Tiv people.

Among the tribes in the Middles Belt, none is as Catholic as the Tiv. That is why even though the DRCM later turned *Nongo u Kristu u Sudan ken Tiv*, (NKST) arrived Tivland first, and taught the Tiv people how to read and write in Tiv, taught the Tiv people to appreciate their *Tivness* and abhor the corrupt culture of the whites; the Tiv embraced Catholicism more readily than NKST doctrine.

Bishop Athanasius Atule Usuh, the first indigenous bishop of Makurdi was a Tiv man (one of the celebrated Seven Sons of Tiv, because they were the first batch of Tiv young men to be ordained Catholic Priests in 1971 at St John's Church in Gboko, the headquarters of Tiv Native Authority) following the first Tiv young man, Father James Akor, who was ordained in 1970 but had to resign shortly afterward. In spite of the negative connotations and stereotype images that label the Tiv people as incapable of accepting the priesthood because it was at variance with their love of the family and progeny, no other tribe in the Middle Belt accepted and embraced Catholicism and the priesthood as the Tiv did, and have done.

---

18 Catholic Church in Nigeria Official Directory (2017-2020), 263.

19 Rubingh, *Sons of Tiv.* 116.

In 1989, when Bishop Usuh took over the diocese, there were the following deaneries: Makurdi, Gboko, Katsina-Ala, Adikpo, Lafia, Keffi and Otukpo. These deaneries represented the major tribal and ethnic delineations that make up the geo-political equation in the region. Otukpo deanery was inhabited predominantly by the Idoma and Igede people; Lafia and Keffi deanerires on the other hand had Alago, Tiv, Eggon, Bassa-Nge, Bassa-Komo, Agatu, Hausa, Fulani, Mada, Gbagyi and other groups down to Uke, Bassa, Mararaba, Karu and of course the Ibo who generally swell the Catholic population abreast with the Tiv. The deaneries of Makurdi, Gboko, Adikpo and Katsina-Ala were predominantly Tiv and represented the strength of the Church in every sense.

The Church in Tivland enjoyed one advantage also: the Tiv people have "a homogenous language, without dialect, spoken and understood by all sons and daughters everywhere. The Tiv have distinctive qualities, including outstanding strength, mental prowess, moral courage, transparent behaviour, hygienic consciousness and environmental cleanliness."[20] These are attributes the Europeans themselves later acknowledged and were led to understand why the Tiv people abhor Islamic practices and culture.

It was therefore a deliberate move by Bishop Usuh to create Otukpo diocese first in 1995 and Lafia second in 2001 to placate the Idoma people and shove aside the huge financial burden of maintaining them, even though the other deaneries of Tiv extraction had more resources, manpower and a vibrant Church. It would take Bishop Usuh a decade to let go the dioceses of Gboko and Katsina-Ala. Among the reasons was the fact that the Tiv people are a homogenous culture and there was that strong sense of solidarity and oneness, and the creation of other dioceses would signal division; in a parochial sense that has been catastrophic: the

[20] Dzurgba, *On the Tiv of Central Nigeria.* 18.

internal divisions of sections and clannish mudslinging led to an implosion that has affected the homogeneity of the Tiv people.

The other factor was the fear that he would be accused of imposing candidates if there were perceived injustices in the selection of candidates for the bishoprics. This dilly-dallying led to further cracks in the fault-lines of political and clannish sentiments that rocked the conversation; and the wait continued. Then the more challenging one: creating one diocese at a time and not two at once. Bishop Usuh knew that if Gboko was created and not Sankera or Katsina-Ala, the people of Katsina-Ala would refuse to join Gboko; and to create Katsina-Ala that had little man-power but wide expanse of land and rich in resources and leave Gboko would be equally problematic.

At a point, the bishop gave up and allowed fate to take its course; then we ramped up the media campaign using different media platforms to encourage him and keep the topic in currency. At the 2004 Catholic Bishops' Conference of Nigeria, held in Makurdi, Benue State, Bishop Usuh formerly made public the request for the new dioceses and was given a strong backing from two prominent Tiv leaders: the then governor of Benue State, George Akume and the Tor Tiv, Alfred Akawe Torkula. In their separate remarks at the conference, both presented their credentials as strong Catholics, and boasted that the political and traditional leadership and the state were in fact Catholic, and that all resources would be made available for the sustenance of these future dioceses.

Many priests did not understand the weight of these presentations and queried the rationale behind the logic. However, this was the ground-swell of impetus Bishop Usuh needed to press for two dioceses simultaneously. He went the extra mile in organising a fund-raiser for the creation of the two dioceses as a strategy to build infrastructure. This is never the protocol in creating a new diocese; but he did it! The diocese raised over a hundred million naira in those days; half of that amount came from Governor George Akume and his friend Governor Jolly Nyame of

Taraba state; it would still be a herculean task for any diocese to raise such a humongous amount at a single event today! Of course the creation of dioceses does not depend on the things we had in place, such as money in the bank and physical structures, but these activities were designed for the local audience; the bishop himself knew what to do.

There was a dramatic shift of attention when Pope Benedict XVI on November 28, 2008 appointed William Avenya as the Auxiliary Bishop of Makurdi Diocese. The jubilation and euphoria that greeted this announcement and the atmosphere that accompanied his consecration on January 24, 2009 were electrifying, indicative of the communion that existed among the Tiv people. Ill-health kept Bishop Usuh away from the diocese and from pastoral activities and the hope of new dioceses faded in the minds of the people, but not in the mind of Bishop Usuh who still believed that the cohesive character of Tiv society had to be maintained.

Just when nobody expected, Pope Benedict XVI announced the creation of Gboko and Katsina-Ala dioceses on December 29, 2012 and Bishop William Avenya was appointed bishop of Gboko and Msgr Peter Adoboh that of Katsina-Ala. Bishop Usuh had accomplished his vision for the Church in Tivland with a masterstroke! The Tiv Church had three indigenous bishops to show for their numerical strength, even though all were from the *Ipusu* bloc of Tivland!

The bishop of Katsina-Ala was installed at Katsina-Ala on February 23, 2013 and the following day the bishop of Gboko was installed at Gboko. On that day, Bishop Usuh reminded the congregation that Adikpo deanery was the only one remaining to be made a diocese out of the deaneries that had made up old Makurdi Diocese, but added that he was not inciting them to start agitating. The following year, the Holy Father Pope Francis who took over from Pope Benedict XVI appointed Msgr Wilfred Chikpa Anagbe Cmf as coadjutor bishop of Makurdi Diocese on July 8, 2014. He was consecrated and succeeded Bishop Usuh on

October 4, 2014 and installed on March 28, 2015. Bishop Anagbe is of Ichongo lineage, the second son of Tiv. Thus, Bishop Usuh balanced the equation so dear to Tiv culture and could then sing his Nunc Dimittis: "At last, all-powerful Master, you give leave to your servant to go in peace, according to your promise." He answered the Lord's call on July 14, 2016, leaving the unfinished symphony of the growth of the Church in Tivland to his successors.

Conclusion

The Catholic Church in Tivland reflects a general picture of the society: Catholic schools for girls and boys, a functional health care sector, and efficient civil service work-force that has provided leadership for the state and Church in northern Nigeria. This effective missionary presence had in time past prevented the advancement of Islam within the region. Unfortunately that cohesion and coordination within the hierarchy of the Church has waned overtime, thus leaving a fragmented population vulnerable to political and sectional manipulation that the Islamist fundamentalists have capitalised on, and as it were, achieving a cheap victory.

The leaders of the Tiv Church never comprehended: the Middle Belt has thus provided the historic meeting-ground for the age-old influences from the north and the east which moulded northern Nigeria, and the more recent economic and religious forces of the west which came largely via Christian missions. This confrontation is now taking place at a heightened tempo and Tivland today finds itself in the heart of this crucible.[21] Armed Fulani herdsmen have continued to kill Tiv people anywhere in Nigeria with impunity, with the hope of scoring the victory Uthman Dan Fodio lost in the hands of the Tiv people during the 1804 jihad.

---

21 Rubingh, *Sons of Tiv.* 53-54.

A homogenous Tiv Church that would have ensured the sustenance of earlier gains made in sustainable human and capital development has been trapped in the thrills of a monolithic culture, self destructive, apathetic and bereft of commitment among the clergy. This lack of strong religious and spiritual leadership from the Catholic Church has become an impetus for the political class to exploit, relativise and undermine religious values and principles, leading to a loss of the sense of the sacred. The political elite no longer see the Church as a sacred institution with the moral authority to hold it and the government accountable for poor performance, corruption and neglect of the electorate.

The education, health and social facilities the Church once provided as an alternative government in Tivland are still the ones the citizens are benefitting from with the government neither providing alternative ones nor sustaining them. Regrettably, even the creation of Adikpo diocese as the late Bishop Usuh indicated has not materialised and the death of Bishop Peter Adoboh of Katsina-Ala in 2020 has affected peace and reconciliation among the restive youth in that area which has had a domino effect in the other regions of Tivland. The advantage the Catholic Church had in Tivland is now challenged by numerous Pentecostal churches and the demographics are changing fast; the Catholic Church has never used its numerical advantage over the years to shape the political leadership, and if its leaders remain stuck in unnecessary and petty squabbles the earlier gains the Church made in Tivland will certainly be erased and it will become a minority in its own house! Although the impact of the Catholic Church in Tivland will be felt for centuries with or without the deliberate interventions on the part of the hierarchy of the Catholic Church in Tivland.

Chapter Four

Catholic Educational Services in Tivland

Tagesa Akpagher[1]

Introduction

Education is a fundamental human right with unquantifiable benefits to individuals and society in general. The Church insists that "All men of every race, condition, and age since they enjoy the dignity of a human being, have an inalienable right to an education."[2] This right is guaranteed in article 26 (1) of the Universal Declaration of human rights.[3] The 1992 Constitution of the Federal Republic of Nigeria, acknowledges the government's fundamental responsibility to provide education in Section 18 (3).[4] Jesus' mandate to the Church was to "teach all nations" (Mt 28:19). Under this mandate, the Church is a teaching instrument that aims to empower people "to develop harmonious-

---

1 Tagesa Akpagher, a priest of the Catholic Diocese of Makurdi, is President of the Tiv Language Studies Association.

2 Second Vatican Council, *Gravissimum Educationis*, #1.

3 Zandy, J. "Universal declaration of human rights." *Radical Teacher*, (2019:113, 54–55). https://doi.org/10.5195/rt.2019.591.

4 *The 1999 Constitution of the Federal Republic of Nigeria.* https://publicofficialsfinancialdisclosure.worldbank.org/sites/fdl/files/assets/law-library-files/Nigeria_Constitution_1999_en.pdf.

ly their physical, moral and intellectual endowments so that they may gradually acquire a mature sense of responsibility in striving endlessly to form their own lives."[5]

The Church as Mother sees her role primarily as that of bringing people to fully participate in human society and derive the maximum benefit in this world and the kingdom as intended by Jesus when he declared, "I have come that you may have life, and have it to the full" (Jn 10:10). Saint Pope John Paul II summarised it in these words: "To her (the Church) was entrusted by her holy Founder the twofold task of giving life to her children and of teaching them and guiding them – both as individuals and nations – with maternal care."[6] In most countries where the Church is engaged in evangelisation through schools, they run the best schools. In the United Kingdom, where I was involved in high school education, the Catholic schools are always the best and were often at full capacity. Although the Church's primary mission is the salvation of souls, it is also deeply concerned for the exigencies of man's daily life.[7] This concern expressed for example by the Church's establishment of schools and hospitals in the evangelisation of the Tiv, the people of Benue Valley.

Pre-colonial Education in Tivland

Through Natural Law, God has provided that life comes without a manual, but humans educate one another for a better social experience on earth. Therefore, the young are taught by those who precede them. The pre-colonial era in Tivland was that of infor-

[5] The Second Vatican Council, *Gravissimum Educationis* #1.

[6] Paul VI, *Mater et Magistra,* #1.

[7] Paul VI, *Mater et Magistra,* #3.

mal education where children's cognitive development followed the process of engagement with cultural and social norms of Tiv world view. Every Tiv child was thoroughly versed in the cultural justice and social systems necessary for social interaction. According to social psychologists, this learning process is achieved when children's cognitive development goes through intensive cultural practices of learning behaviours and interacting with the environment as they grow up. In this way, learning usually involves interaction and changes in the neurons that are inborn and the synapses formed after birth, thereby enabling increasingly complex and efficient thoughts in cognitive development.[8]

The Tiv of the pre-colonial era educated their young through social interaction and norms and cultural practices following the social identity theory.[9] As a collectivist culture, as opposed to an individualistic culture, the Tiv taught their children social norms that value communal experiences. Road construction was always a communal function, and even farm work and building constructions were communal activities.[10] Child-rearing was as communal as any other social activity such that all children were taught that community interest trumps individual interest. This was exemplified in the naming of children, *Ityôhemba* (the community is supreme), *Ityôngi* (the community exists – meaning that one should be mindful of his limitations), *Ityôver* (the community has blessed), *Ityôakura* (the community will protect), and so on.

---

8 Laura Berk, *Development through the Life Span.* Seventh Edition. (Boston: Pearson, 2018).

9 Miller J, Das R, Chakravarthy S. "Culture and the Role of Choice in Agency" *Journal of Personality and Social Psychology* (2011) 101(1) 46-61 DOI: 10.1037/a0023330.

10 H. C. Boucher, & Maslach, C. "Culture and Individuation: The Role of Norms and Self-Construals." *Journal of Social Psychology*, (2009) *149* (6), 677–693.

Education was based on three main socialising agents, the family, peer groups, and the community. In psychology, Group Socialization Theory has identified peer groups as the dominant socialising agent in developing children's lives.[11] Community-based organisations such as youth associations, market women associations, and age-grade systems were used in socialisation in Tivland. The age-grade system was an effective means of social control since there was no central authority in Tivland. This system stratified society into groups where values were learned and discipline enforced. As a collectivist culture, the system worked well, and Tiv society was prosperous and joyful as people supported one another in their wealth creation.

The Church's Intervention in Education

The Benue valley is situated in the Middle Belt of Nigeria and does not have any sea coast. Therefore, the European explorers did not make early contact with the Tiv until much later in the late 19th century. Richard Lander, an English explorer, only discovered the great Benue River and was later explored by Lt. Col. Trenchard.[12] Even after the initial contact, notable engagement was delayed because the British found it frustrating to deal with the segmented system of governance practiced by the Tiv.[13]

They resisted to be subdued under the indirect rule of the Northern Emirs. Even though the British had superior weapons,

---

[11] D. L. Vandell, "Parents, peer groups, and other socialising influences." *Developmental Psychology*, (2000) *36* (6), 699–710. https://doi.org/10.1037/0012-1649.36.6.699.

[12] Kirk-Greene, A. "Expansion on the Benue 1830-1900." *Journal of the Historical Society of Nigeria,* (1958) (3), 215-237. Retrieved August 25, 2021, from http://www.jstor.org/stable/41856634.

[13] Andrew Boyle, *Trenchard Man of Vision.* (St. James' Place London: Collins, 1962).

they could not subdue the Tiv people and had to retreat several times and conquer other ethnic nationalities as they advanced towards Southern Nigeria. Without a king or central authority, the Tiv could still organise a resistance strong enough to put the British off.[14]

Since the development of the African colonial territories was not a direct policy of the British, Tivland did not benefit from British-established public schools until the missionaries arrived. Therefore, the first school in Tivland was opened in 1905 at Wanune by Rev. G. P. Barkery of the Dutch Missionaries. This school later became the Benue Provisional School in 1952 before becoming Government College Katsina-Ala in 1960.[15]

The Catholic presence in Tivland only began in 1889 when it was part of the Eastern Nigerian Prefecture Apostolic manned by German Holy Ghost fathers. They had great success opening schools for education and evangelisation under Shanahan. When the Benue area was raised to the Prefecture Apostolic in 1934, the team of priests under Shanahan began to replicate what gave them success in Eastern Nigeria. They began establishing schools wherever they established new missions.[16]

Thus, the first Mission at Udei came with a school in 1924. After that, schools began to appear in different places, St Theresa's Naka in 1931, St Joseph's Korinya, in 1934 and Mount St Michael's

---

14 David Craig Dorward, "The Development of the British Colonial Administration among the Tiv, 1900-1949." *African Affairs.* (1969) ***68*** *(273): 316–333. doi:10.1093/oxford journals.afraf.a095924. JSTOR 720655.*

15 Newsdiary.com access August 25, 2021, from www.newsdiary.com.

16 William Avenya, "The Role of the Clergy in Educational Development in Makurdi Diocese." in *Catholic Diocese of Makurdi at 50: A Celebration of Service to Humanity.* Ed. Shagbaor F. Wegh (Makurdi: Selfers Academic Press Ltd, 2010).

Aliade in 1953.[17] St James Junior Seminary began first in Otukpo in 1955 and had an exciting journey. It was moved to Keffi in 1957 and then to Makurdi in 1971.[18] The school continued its journey to Aliade in 1986 and finally settled at Yandev in Gboko in 1993. On its Makurdi premises stands the Divine Mercy Junior Seminary, which Bishop Wilfred Chikpa Anagbe CMF established in 2016.

The Church's commitment to the establishment of schools comes from her firm conviction that schools have special significance in the life of individuals and communities:

> Among all educational instruments, the school has particular importance. It is designed to develop with special care the intellectual faculties and form the ability to judge rightly, to hand on the cultural legacy of previous generations, foster a sense of values, and prepare for professional life. Between pupils of different talents and backgrounds, it promotes friendly relations and fosters a spirit of mutual understanding.[19]

The Catholic schools in Tivland did precisely that, providing good education and preparing people to take up leadership positions in the national life of Nigeria. The late Tor Tiv, Alfred Akawe Torkula, Late Professor David Ker, Dr Iyorchia Ayu, Lucy Aluor, Dorathy Kpojime, Elizabeth Kpojime, Justice Margaret Igbetar, Rebecca Apedzan, Patricia Ashi Aondo-Akaa, Elizabeth-Mary Nguumbur Shuluwa are some products of Catholic schools in Tivland. This

---

17 Moses Orhungur, "Education as a Tool for Evangelisation." in *Catholic Diocese of Makurdi at 50: A Celebration of Service to Humanity*. Ed. Shagbaor F. Wegh (Makurdi: Selfers Academic Press Ltd, 2010).

18 Wegh F. Shagbaor, "The Emergence of the Catholic Diocese of Makurdi." in *Catholic Diocese of Makurdi at 50: A Celebration of Service to Humanity*. Ed. Shagbaor F. Wegh (Makurdi: Selfers Academic Press Ltd, 2010).

19 Second Vatican Council, *Gravissimum Educationis*, #5.

"educational approach (to evangelisation) adopted by the Church created thousands of jobs and empowered people to attain their existential ends."[20]

These Schools were a veritable tool for evangelisation as the Catholic faith was taught, and some of the students became Catechists and Church Leaders. As many as 250 men came out as priests and bishops. Late Bishop Athanasius Usuh of Makurdi Diocese, Bishop William Avenya of Gboko Diocese, Late Bishop Peter Adoboh of Katsina-Ala diocese, and John Cardinal Onaiyekan, the former Archbishop of Abuja, are all products of Catholic education in Tivland. When Pope Francis said, "with Christ, joy is constantly born anew"[21] he meant that every encounter with the Gospel brings great joy as it is a liberating Good News. The encounter between the Gospel and Tivland has brought boundless joy.

The unique contribution of Catholic education services in Tivland is the discipline and high academic standards. These bring high achievements that produce socially desirable values. This was possible in Tivland because Catholic education services promoted a culture of free inquiry and engagement with contemporary advancements and local culture. Catholic education inculcated in the Tiv the values of honest expression and a unique work ethic to give the best for the common good. This is exemplified in the work that products of Catholic education do. For instance, in the short time that Rev. Fr Moses Orshio Adasu served as the governor of Benue state in 1992, he was able to establish a university and many other projects of high economic value to the state. The State University is now the pride of the state and has educated many sons and daughters of Tivland.

20 See Moses Orhungur, "Education as a Tool for Evangelisation."

21 Pope Francis. Apostolic Exhortation, *Evangelii Gaudium* #1.

Education is not merely a scientific acquisition of knowledge but a holistic human formation that equips individuals to function in society and contribute to society's development.[22] Moti argues that "the church goes into schools and establishes her own schools because she considers them as a privileged means of promoting the formation of the whole person."[23]

The Church's educational engagement is always in partnership with the state which has the primary responsibility for the education of citizens as enshrined in Chapter two of the 1999 Nigerian constitution.[24] The constitution notes, "Government shall direct its policy towards ensuring that there are equal and adequate educational opportunities at all levels (and that) government shall and when practicable provide free, compulsory and universal primary education; free secondary education; free university education and free adult literacy program" (Section 18 (1), (3)a, b, c, d).[25] Therefore, government interventions and grants to Church schools is not charity, but the fulfillment of state responsibility. Like it is done in the United Kingdom and elsewhere, this is not just a desirable approach in Benue State but a necessity for the right of the Benue child to receive an education.

Indeed, the government take-over of schools in Nigeria in the late 1970s was the biggest mistake in the history of education in Nigeria, whose consequences still linger. Although, in Benue state,

---

22 Juvova, A., Chudy, S., Neumeister, P., Plischke, J., & Kvintova, J. "Reflection of Constructivist Theories in Current Educational Practice." *Universal Journal of Educational Research*, (2015) *3* (5), 345–349.

23 James Shagba Moti, "The Catholic Ethos in Private and Public Schools in Makurdi Diocese." in *Catholic Diocese of Makurdi at 50: A Celebration of Service to Humanity*. Ed. Shagbaor F. Wegh (Makurdi: Selfers Academic Press Ltd, 2010).

24 *The 1999 Constitution of the Federal Republic of Nigeria.*

25 *The 1999 Constitution of the Federal Republic of Nigeria.* Chapter 2, Section 18 (1) and (3).

the government continued with a partial grants-in-aid to schools, in the payment of teachers' salaries, this sustained the partnership of Church and State in the provision of education but aspects have continued to suffer neglect.

The introduction of the Universal Primary Education (UPE) by the government was intended to make education accessible to all children irrespective of the social-economic status of their families. However, management failures, diversion of recourses and embezzlement affected primary education, and today there are more children out of school than ever before in the history of Nigeria. According to UNICEF, Nigeria has the highest number of children out of school in the whole world. The UNICEF report of 2018 says there are between 10.5million and 13.4million Nigerian children out of school.[26] Catholic education can reverse this if given the necessary financial support by the government.

Remarkably, the Catholic Church for her part often establishes schools with funds raised by her poor members from the pews. When the schools become successful, the same Church members cannot afford the high school fees that are charged. Yet, successful school administration requires considerable financial capital to drive up achievement levels. Therefore, charging high school fees becomes inevitable. However, when the government takes up its responsibility of providing education by bearing the cost of running the schools, it will become easier for children of all backgrounds to access quality education in Catholic schools. It is the right of all children to be educated by the State. If the Church is providing a service that is the government's responsibility, then it is morally reprehensible for the government to impose taxes on Catholic schools as currently obtains.

[26] UNICEF. https://www.unicef.org/nigeria/education.

The Way Forward

Education must be seen as human formation rather than a mere nursery for employees. Cultural and social values and individual and communal identities are established in one's life through education. In order to raise children who will become future policymakers on crucial issues like the environment, governance, economy, etc., school administration and curriculum must change to address the challenges that different scientific disciplines are throwing up. Therefore, educational psychologists call for holistic and accessible education that prepares students to find solutions for life challenges in creative and innovative ways.

Inclusive Education

Catholic education is based on the premise that all children have a right to education because of their human dignity. Therefore, special consideration is given to children with special needs and with learning difficulties of varying degrees so that they too can access good quality education. The Church has established a school for the hearing and sight-impaired at Vandeikya, while the government established a similar one at Aliade and Ameladu. However, Children with special needs do not live in isolation but alongside non-disabled children in society. Therefore, modern policymakers in education prefer to educate special needs children in an inclusive environment.[27] The National Policy on Education 2008 in Nigeria advocated that special needs children should not be educated separately but in inclusive classrooms where they

---

27 M. A. Lamport, Graves, L., & Ward, A. "Special Needs Students in Inclusive Classrooms: for Learners with Emotional and Behavioral Disabilities." *European Journal of Business and Social Sciences*, (2012) *1* (5), 54–69.

learn alongside non-disabled children without any restrictions.[28] Ajuwon argues that inclusive education has many benefits, such as learning social skills, developing appropriate language skills, building self-confidence in special needs children, and increasing society's awareness and acceptability of human conditions. [29]

Thus, the Catholic education services in Tivland must retrain its teachers to understand inclusive education and support children with special needs to access the curriculum the same way as the other children. Special needs of learners should not be treated as pathologies needing a medical cure. Schools should have psychologists that will test every child and profile them according to their needs to be well supported in inclusive classrooms. In the past, hyperactive children were classified as stubborn and unteachable, just as dyslexic children were considered "blockheads" and were beaten when they could not recognise alphabets. Trained special needs teachers will be able to recognise these conditions and support the children who have them.

Special needs teachers will better manage inclusive classrooms not only with challenged children, but with Gifted and Talented children whose IQ is well above average and have higher learning expectations. This group must be challenged at the appropriate level to sustain their engagement and keep them motivated. Giving them differentiated learning activities in lessons will keep them out of mischief and extend their learning.[30] Gifted and Talented

---

28 Federal Ministry of Education. *National Policy on Education.* (2008). https://education.gov.ng/wp-content/uploads/2020/06/NATIONAL-POLICY-ON-EDUCATION.pdf.

29 P. M. Ajuwon, "Inclusive Education for Students with Disabilities in Nigeria: Benefits, Challenges and Policy Implications." *International Journal of Special Education*, (2008) *23* (3), 11–16.

30 B. Swan, Coulombe-Quach, X.-L., Huang, A., Godek, J., Becker, D., & Zhou, Y. "Meeting the Needs of Gifted and Talented Students." *Journal of Advanced Academics*, (2015). *26* (4), 294–319. Retrieved from 10.1177/1932202X15603366.

children can easily be bored when the teacher devotes time to low-ability learners, hyperactive attention-deficient learners, or those with emotional needs. Managing all these groups in an inclusive lesson requires specialised skills. Catholic education in Tivland must be willing to commit resources to retraining teachers for their professional development. There are many new teaching and learning trends, and teachers cannot remain with archaic teaching strategies that have become obsolete and ineffective.

Catholic Education should train teachers to move away from rote learning where children are loaded with information and taught to memorize it. New ways of teaching and learning emphasize developing critical thinking skills where children can solve problems and discover new knowledge. Lev Vygotsky's theory of learning talks about the *Zone of Proximal Development,* which represents the space between the child's ability and the external support from the teacher.[31] Using this method, teachers design problem-solving learning activities that challenge students to solve problems independently, creatively, and innovatively according to individual abilities. The learners are only supported where they fall short, and those who are low-ability learners or special needs learners are supported using the scaffolding approach. They are given help that is gradually withdrawn until they can stand on their own.[32]

Appropriate levels of investment must be made in education so that infrastructure can be well maintained with modern learning equipment to motivate both learners and teachers. According to the psychological theory of motivation, the environment is one of

---

31 P. Van Geert, "A dynamic systems model of basic developmental mechanisms: Piaget, Vygotsky, and beyond." *Psychological Review*, (1998). *105*(4), 634–677.

32 A. F. Hadwin, Wozney, L., & Pontin, O. "Scaffolding the appropriation of self-regulatory activity: A socio-cultural analysis of changes in teacher-student discourse about a graduate research portfolio." *Instructional Science*, (2005) *33* (5–6), 413–450. https://doi.org/10.1007/s11251-005-1274-7.

the essential elements in human motivation.[33] In this way, pedagogy moves into a self-regulated area of personalised learning where learners gradually take more control of their learning.

Open Day – The Church and educational psychologists have acknowledged the critical role of parents in the education of children.[34] Parents are among the socialising agents in the developing child's life alongside peers, school, and the community. Therefore, Catholic Education in Tivland must encourage the greater involvement of parents in the educational process, as children are more motivated and go on to achieve better when their parents show interest in their learning experience. Parents' involvement in education modifies children's learning behaviour for higher achievements. This involvement could be done through *Open Days* when parents are invited to the school to meet with their wards in front of individual subject teachers to receive feedback on how their wards are doing and learn what they can do at home to support their learning. It is not a time for confrontation but an honest assessment and appreciation of the learning process. Open Days can also help the children modify their behaviour at home.

The Need for a Catechetical Institute

The Church's engagement in education is not just the provision of social services but also the development of human persons and the evangelisation of peoples. The early missionaries established schools to develop people and to train agents of evangelisation. This paid off well as many people emerged as Catechists and Church Leaders who continuously sustain the evangelical work of

---

33 R. G. Geen, "Human motivation: New perspectives on old problems." in *The G. Stanley Hall lecture series, Vol. 4.* (Washington, DC, US: American Psychological Association, 1984, 9–57). https://doi.org/10.1037/10089-001.

34 Second Vatican Council. *Gravissimum Educationis*, #6.

the Church in rural areas. The success story of the Church in Tivland will never be complete without the contribution of Catechists and Voluntary Catechists whose number is growing by the day and whose services are becoming more and more central to the pastoral life of the Church. For them to serve their Ecclesial communities well, they need to be adequately trained and equipped. Therefore, it is time to establish a Catechetical Institute in Tivland to cater to the growing number of laypersons involved in the Church's work of evangelisation.

The Need for a Catholic University in Tivland

Over the years, Catholic Education Services in Tivland has recorded tremendous successes and has brought about positive social change in Nigeria. This must be sustained and improved upon in our generation. During the Second Synod of the Catholic Diocese of Makurdi, it was resolved that the time has come for the diocese to establish a tertiary institution to move forward on the gains that have been achieved at the primary and secondary levels of education by the Church. It is ten years since then, and we have just concluded the third synod. Perhaps the time to act is now, with the commitment that Most Rev. Wilfred Chikpa Anagbe, CMF, the Bishop of Makurdi, has shown that there can be no better time to begin such a venture than now in developing the diocese. The diocese of Gboko is already taking steps towards realising the dream of a Catholic University in Tivland, as work has already commenced at the proposed site at Vandeikya.

Conclusion

The Christian faith first came into Tivland through the work of Dutch Protestant missionaries. The Catholic Church was a late arrival, but she has more followers today than any other denomination in Tivland. This is due mainly to the hard work that has been achieved in her educational services in Tivland. We can genuinely refer to the Gospel as 'Good News' for the Tiv people because of the positive impact it has made in their lives. The Church cannot rest on her oars. We must continue to strengthen the capacity of the same system that has brought many gains for the Church in Tivland.

Let those who are beneficiaries of Catholic Education Services give back to the system to improve it for the benefit of future generations. This includes those who have been bishops, priests, religious, and those in prominent positions in society. They must influence educational policy at every level in order to bring about positive change in Catholic education. In this way, indigent members of the society can have access to education, and the Church's mission of evangelisation can continue.

Chapter Five

Catholic Healthcare Services in Tivland

Michael I. Dogo[1]

Introduction

I came so that they may have life and have it to the full (Jn 10:10).

Healthcare was a key approach by Christian missionaries in gaining acceptance in Tivland. The World Council of Churches has maintained that health and healing are not just medical issues. Other dimensions like the political, social, economic, cultural, and the spiritual are all involved:

> Although the "health industry" is producing and using progressively sophisticated and expensive technology, the increasingly obvious fact is that most of the world's health problems cannot be best addressed in this way. It is an acknowledged fact that the number one cause of disease in the world is poverty, which is ultimately the result of oppression, exploitation and war. Providing immunisations, medicines, and even health education by standard methods cannot significantly ameliorate illness due to poverty.[2]

---

1 Rev. Fr Michael Dogo, is a priest of the Catholic Diocese of Gboko, who serves as the Diocesan Health Coordinator and oversees the health institutions of the diocese.

2 World Council of Churches, *Healing and Wholeness*, as quoted by Gabriel T. Wankar, "Healing as Constitutive of Jesus' Mission Handed to the Church" in *International*

This view of health and wellness has informed the engagement of the Catholic Church in its healthcare delivery efforts besides evangelisation among Tiv.

In the over a hundred years now of its presence among the Tiv, the Catholic Church has significantly contributed to healthcare, seeing it as a basic need and invested heavily in it, beginning with the expatriates and followed by the indigenous clergy, who have lived up to the task and expanded the scope of healthcare delivery. An increased number of hospitals, clinics, and primary healthcare centers are scattered across Tivland, courtesy of the indigenous-led Catholic Church. These centers actively take part in preventive, curative, and even rehabilitative health. However, considering the level of poverty in the land, it becomes a challenge to marry quality health care and affordability.

Indeed, the Catholic Church sees health care as a continuation of the healing ministry of Jesus Christ. Thus, the Church's healthcare ministry also sees a human person not just as a patient with whatever ailment but as a reflection of love.[3] This ministry is concerned very significantly with the sacredness of life and its transmission.

The Tiv, domiciled in the middle belt region of Nigeria, were ordinarily known to be very resistant to foreign cultures and traditions. Anything the Tiv people were not used to was not to be accepted. As much as they were very receptive, they would not condone what contradicted what they knew or practiced. They were wary of newcomers. Wegh captures it thus:

Review of Mission Volume 109. Number 1 (May 2020), 23.

3 Gboko Diocesan Health Care Initiative: Policies and Operational Guidelines,(2020) Gboko; G.D.P.P. (ii).

> Furthermore, the Tiv had a very strong antipathy for anything coming from southern Nigeria and that would not augur well for a mission launched from Ogoja…the Tiv were very wary of any newcomer so it would be no use making rare and rapid appearance amongst them if we wish to gain their confidence and persuade them[4]

This disbelief in a foreign culture by the Tiv man included orthodox medicine, Western education, Western religion, and all that was believed to be alien to his usual way of life. His belief in the potency of traditional medicine of *kwaghsorun man akombo*[5]was seen by him to be superior to any form of treatment.[6] For the Tiv people at that time, this was not to be contested.

With the coming of the missionaries and the introduction of orthodox medicine, the Tiv people gradually began to embrace modern healthcare, and bit by bit, dispensaries, maternity homes, clinics, and even hospitals began to spring up in different parts of Tivland under the canopy of the old Makurdi Diocese which birthed the Integrated Health Program (I.H.P.).

The Church's Thoughts on Health

According to the World Health Organisation (WHO), health is "a state of complete physical, mental and social well-being and

---

4 Shagbaor F. Wegh, "The Emergence of the Catholic Diocese of Makurdi," in *Catholic Diocese of Makurdi at 50: A Celebration of Service and Humanity, (*Makurdi; Selfers Academic Press, 2010), 28.

5 A Tiv traditional rite is meant for healing and cleansing, which in most cases combines herbs and rituals with an animal. Cosmo-supernatural Powers Represented in Emblems are also featured.

6 James S. Moti and Shagbaor F. Wegh, *An Encounter between Tiv Religion and Christianity*. (Enugu: Snap Press, 2001), 25-27.

not merely the absence of disease and infirmity."[7] This definition is, however, seen by many as grossly inadequate. Scholars opine that any reasonable definition of health must encompass the various dimensions of the physical, spiritual, moral, psychological, and social dimensions of a human being.

In sync with the understanding of wellness and health by the World Council of Churches, the Catholic Church believes that health is not only physical and/ or mental well-being, but includes the social and spiritual and other dimensions as well.[8] In effect, healthcare demands addressing the medical needs of person as well as his spiritual, psychological needs, which involves working for justice, peace, and the integrity of creation. The Church has done a lot to ensure that healing does not only come to the human soul alone but the body as well, thereby living Christ's injunction that says; "*I have come that they may have life and have it to the full.*" Thus, basic needs like the provision of portable water in the rural areas, access roads, and improved farm techniques are key components of the Church's healthcare interventions as disease preventive strategies and healthy living.

Often, the Church's health care is delivered by an interdisciplinary team of agents and professionals, who combine health and social service provisions enunciated in the elaborate body of Catholic social teaching. These services are delivered by agents who are professionals in medicine, dentistry, nursing, pharmacy, and allied health sciences. They employ healthcare equipment and services, pharmaceuticals, biotechnology and life sciences, providers of healthcare plans, and home healthcare. The *Catechism of the Catholic Church* has summarizes the Church's underlying

---

7 Definition of health by WHO: retrieved from https://www.google.com/search?q=who+definition+of+health&ie=utf-8&oe=utf-8.

8 Wankar, "Healing as Constitutive of Jesus' Mission Handed to the Church" 22.

philosophy in respect to healthcare: *"Life and physical health are precious gifts entrusted to us by God. We must take reasonable care of them, taking into account the needs of others and the common good."*[9]

The Birth of Catholic Healthcare Services in Tivland

With the perceived difficulty in making the Tiv people accept the new way of life that was to be introduced to them, healthcare provision, apart from being the Church's concern for people, became one of the pathways used to gain easy access and acceptance in Tivland. Alumuku, quoted by Torwel in *Catholic Diocese of Makurdi at 50;* says:

> Medical units and maternities were a sign of the Church's concern for the people. So it was hoped that the older people who saw the usefulness of the medical services offered would eventually become Christians. This mission element endeared the Church to many people who saw the Church as a sign of hope and mercy.[10]

Many people and communities in Tivland have benefited from the health facilities provided by the Church. Aneke in Udoo says the earliest healthcare providers in the land were a joint approach between the government and the medical missionaries from whence the system grew.

The earliest healthcare service delivery in Tivland was a joint approach between the government and medical missionaries who

9 Catechism of the Catholic Church, Retrieved from https://www.google.com/url?q=https://www.catholicculture.org/culture/library/catechism/.

10 Vitalis Torwel, "A Multimedia Approach to Evangelisation in Makurdi Diocese: Some Practical Issues" in *Catholic Diocese of Makurdi at 50: A Celebration of Service and Humanity.* Ed. Shagbaor F. Wegh (Makurdi; Selfers Academic Press, 2010), 170-171.

came to deliver healthcare services to the sick and disabled in the designated centers in the Old Makurdi Diocese. Those centers eventually became health posts to control communicable diseases such as leprosy, tuberculosis, cholera, measles, and other diseases.[11]

The journey of healthcare provision in Tivland by the Catholic Church, according to records, started with the takeover of a miniature railway clinic by the Holy Ghost Parish, Makurdi. This was to become Holy Ghost Dispensary before the Benue-Plateau government again took it over to become General Hospital Makurdi and subsequently, the Federal Medical Centre, Makurdi in 1995. A statement published on the F.M.C.M. page says:

> The hospital, which is now referred to as Federal Medical Centre (F.M.C.) Makurdi started in 1927 as a small railway clinic to offer first-aid treatment to railway workers. It was subsequently taken over by the Catholic Mission in 1940 as a dispensary. The defunct Government of Benue-Plateau State acquired it in 1967 as a General Hospital. In its desire to enable every state in the country to access tertiary healthcare, the Federal Government of Nigeria acquired it in 1995 as Federal Medical Centre.[12]

Today, the Federal Medical Center Makurdi has remained one of the state's outstanding tertiary healthcare providers, and the church shares in this glory.

Another early health entry into Tivland was the Korinya experience of 1955, with St Joseph's C.H.C., Korinya. However, a significant turnaround of the Catholic Church healthcare delivery

---

11 A Udoo "The Role of the Catholic Church in the Development of Makurdi Diocesan Area of Benue State." (Unpublished Thesis, 2019) retrieved from http://bsuir.bsum.edu.ng/bitstream/11409/664/1/UDOO%20ANDIIR.pdf.

12 "Historical Background of the Federal Medical Center Makurdi." Accessed from https://fmcmakurdi.gov.ng/historical-background.

was the Adikpo experience of 1966. The Adikpo experience was both rudimentary and sacrificial. It was borne out of need and zeal. The locals sacrificed just like the missionary sisters and priests did, and all these were done in joy and gladness, which birthed what is today known as St Monica's Hospital Adikpo. This hospital will therefore become the story of the Integrated Health Programme (I.H.P.) and that of the entire Tiv-speaking area of the Old Makurdi Diocese. This is apart from the establishment of St Joseph's C.H.C. Korinya and the partnership between the government and the missionaries in healthcare delivery which was short-lived.

In 1954, the housecraft Women Training Centre, the Holy Rosary Convent was established at Adikpo and was run by the Holy Rosary Sisters.[13] Admitting both married and unmarried women from Benue and Kogi axes into this institution opened the flood gates for the influx of people into the small hilly village of Adikpo. The Sisters did a commendable job in grooming the young ladies into refined and God-fearing young women. This attracted more people, and the community gradually began to expand. With the expansion came the needs of the people, and health was a top priority. A publication on the website of St Monica's Hospital Adikpo posits that:

> With the amicable attitude of the Holy Rosary Sisters towards their students and the women in the villages around them generally, requests started coming in from the villages, particularly from the pregnant women, for natal or childbirth care and transport services to the hospital in emergencies.[14]

---

[13] Joy Abu, "The Evangelisation Strides of the Holy Rosary Sister in Makurdi Diocese"in *Catholic Diocese of Makurdi at 50: A Celebration of Service and Humanity,* (Makurdi; Selfers Academic Press, 2010), 48-49.

[14] "About St Monica's Hospital Adikpo." Retrieved from http://www.stmonicashospitaladikpo.org/

Even as these emergencies were coming, it was becoming quite difficult for the missionaries to cope with the demands of the locals due to the frequency of the demands, the crisis-prone area of Obudu, which made it quite unsafe and tiring, and the tedious distance to N.K.S.T Hospital Mkar, which was the only alternative at the moment. The statement further adds that:

> The nearest hospital was Sacred Heart Hospital, Obudu in Cross River State, but because of the sporadic communal clashes between Cross River and Benue, it was not always possible to rush women to Obudu. Therefore, it was safer to rush them to N.K.S.T. Hospital Mkar, which is about 56 kilometers away from Adikpo. With the added health problems of the students, which the Sisters had to attend to by rushing them to the hospital, the Sisters' only vehicle became more or less an ambulance.[15]

With the dearth of public transportation at that time, the pressure kept mounting for a health facility to be drawn closer to the people, and in 1964, the Catholic community formally requested a health facility in Adikpo. The publication continues:

> "The Reverend Fathers were not left out. Apart from their huge workload which they had in visiting Christians Catechumens in the out-stations in the bush for baptismal examinations and administration of the Sacraments, they were surrounded by the people with serious problems. In most cases, they were emergencies that had to be helped to the hospital to save lives. It must be remembered that public transportation was very rare in those days. It happened that in 1964 the Superior-General, Mother Gabriel was in Adikpo on her routine tour of visiting Holy Rosary Sisters in the Diocese. The Catholic lay community in Adikpo, in co-operation with the priests and the sisters requested the Mother-Superior for a Clinic/Maternity for Adikpo as a special case."[16]

---

15 Ibid.

16 Ibid.

Upon the approval of this request, the Catholic Women Organisation (C.W.O.) was tasked to gather sand to build the new maternity after a rainstorm had blown the temporary abode used for this purpose. The hospital page further captures thus:

> Sure enough, God, in His infinite mercy and goodness, granted this request. In 1966 a small Clinic/Maternity was opened. Rev. Sister Alice Power (S.M. Carthage) was assigned to take charge of the unit. She took over a classroom in the vacated primary school, using it as a maternity unit. Initially, cardboard cartons were used as cots. Unfortunately, a storm came and blew the roof off the classroom, which served as maternity. The babies were moved in cardboard cartons like kittens to a round hut as their new maternity. The Parish Priest, Rev. Fr A. O Sullivan, threw a challenge to the Catholic Women Organisation (C.W.O.) to rise and bring sand for their long-awaited maternity. The C.W.O., under the leadership of Mama Anna and her Vice Chairperson, the late Madam Maria Ikpato, accepted the challenge, and in no time, there was enough sand and . A new maternity block was erected on the present site; it is now known as "Pediatrics Ward."In 1968 Rev. Sister Riona joined Alice Power, the first staff of the Clinic/Maternity.[13]

This birthed St Monica's Hospital Adikpo, which also served as a fulcrum for the emergence of other health facilities, explaining why numerous Catholic health facilities are found around this axis. Until the creation of Katsina-Ala and Gboko Dioceses, the Integrated Health Program held sway in the entire Tivland regarding the provision of healthcare services.

With the creation of the two dioceses, Katsina-Ala came up with the Katsina-Ala Diocesan Integrated Health Care Services (K.D.I.H.C.S.), while Gboko Diocese took off with the Gboko Diocesan Health Care Initiative (G.D.H.C.I.). The Integrated Health Program (I.H.P.), Catholic Diocese of Makurdi, Katsina-Ala Diocesan Integrated Health Care Services (K.D.I.H.C.S.), and Gboko Diocesan Health Care Initiative (G.D.H.C.I.) are the organisations saddled with the provision of health care services in the three Dioceses respectively.

The types of services rendered by the Catholic Church through the three various health care initiatives, their secretariats and health facilities, are four in nature; these are preventive, curative, rehabilitative, and referral. The preventive service delivery is rendered by the primary health care component of the service providing organs of the dioceses in Tivland. The activities include immunisation, health education, treatment of minor ailments, care of the physically handicapped, referral, and community mobilisation. At the same time, those of curative produced by secondary health facilities include treatment of both major and minor illnesses, surgery, immunisation, health education, and referral. Both carry out care, treatment, and support to orphans and vulnerable children (OVC) and people living with HIV/AIDS in collaboration with other Implementing Partners (IPs) and parishes in which the facilities are situated.

For the assignment of the various levels of treatment, the Catholic healthcare services adopts the health tier system of Primary Health Care (P.H.C.), Comprehensive Health Centers (C.H.C.s) Hospitals, and medical centers. The Catholic Church health care system is as interested in healing the soul as it is in healing the body. To this end, chaplaincies are established at these health facilities where the priests (chaplains) offer counseling and sacraments to our patients.

The Integrated Health Program (I.H.P.) in Makurdi Diocese covers four (4) local government areas. These are, Makurdi, Guma, Gwer East and Gwer West. I.H.P. has one Medical Centre, three Hospitals, one (1) C.H.C., and six (6) P.H.C.s. The health facilities overseen by the I.H.P. are listed below with their locations and years of establishment.

S/N	NAME OF FACILITY	LOCATION	YEAR OF EST.
1	Bishop Murray Medical Centre	High Level, Makurdi LG	1969
2	St Vincent's Hospital	Aliade, Gwer East LG	1975
3	St Matthias' Hospital	Naka, Gwer West LG	1983
4	St Gregory's Hospital	Ikpayongo, Gwer East L.G	2005
5	St Francis P.H.C.	Agagbe, Gwer West LG	1994
6	Fr John Ikponko P.H.C.	Uhembe, Makurdi LG	2004
7	St Michael's P.H.C.	Agasha, Guma LG	2005
8	Sacred Heart P.H.C. Udei,	Guma LG	2005
9	St Athanasius' P.H.C.	Gbajimba Guma LG	2007
10	Divine Mercy C.H.C.	Daudu, Guma LG	2015
11	St Veronica's P.H.C.	Aondoana, Gwer West LG	2019

Facilities under I.H.P. in Makurdi Diocese. Source:[17]

The Katsina-Ala Diocesan Integrated Health Care Services (K.D.I.H.C.S.), which houses the health services in that axis, has under its watch one (1) Hospital, one (1) C.H.C., and five (5) P.H.C.s as shown below. It is to be noted that the area administered by K.D.I.H.S., just like the Diocese, comprises three (3) local governments: Katsina-Ala, Logo, and Ukum.

[17] A. Udoo, "The Role of the Catholic Church in the Development of Makurdi Diocesan Area of Benue State."

S/N	NAME OF FACILITY	LOCATION	YEAR OF EST.
1	St Anthony's Hospital	Zaki-Biam, Ukum LG	1984
2	St Mary's P.H.C.	Chito, Ukum LG	1995
3	St Margaret's P.H.C.	Tor-Donga K/Ala LG	2005
4	Holy Ghost P.H.C.	Abeda, K/Ala LG	1984
5	St Thomas P.H.C.	Afia, Logo LG	2000
6	Fr Christopher P.H.C.	Kyodo Ukum LG	2015
7	Bishop Peter Adoboh Memorial Clinic	Katsina-Ala, K/Ala LG	2020

Facilities under K.D.I.H.C.S. in Katsina-Ala Diocese.[18]

Gboko Diocese, just like its organ, the G.D.H.C.I., covers seven (7) local government areas. These Local government areas include Buruku, Gboko, Konshisha, Kwande, Tarka, Ushongo, and Vandeikya. As the responsible health organ for Gboko Diocese, G.D.H.C.I. currently oversees twenty-six (26) health facilities. These include four (4) Hospitals, four (4) C.H.C.s and eighteen (18) P.H.C.s. Plans have been concluded to commission two (2) more facilities, one in Awajir, Konshisha local government area and another in Garagboughul, Buruku Local Government area.

[18] Telephone conversation with KDIHCS M&E and Administrative Secretary (July 2021).

S/N	NAME OF FACILITY	LOCATION	YEAR OF EST.
1	St Monica's Hospital	Adikpo, Kwande LG	1966
2	St Thomas' Hospital	Ihugh, Vandeikya LG	1974
3	St John's Hospital	Gboko Central Gboko LG	2020
4	St Elizabeth's Hospital	Vandeikya, Vandeikya LG	1968
5	St Christopher's C.H.C.	Wannune, Tarkaa LG	1987
6	St Joseph's C.H.C.	Korinya, Konshisha LG	1965
7	St Veronica's C.H.C.	Agidi, Gboko LG	1987
8	36 Martyrs	C.H.C. Mbape, Kwande LG	2006
9	St Martins De Pores	Abwa, Buruku LG	2004
10	St Augustine's P.H.C.	Ayana, Kwande LG	1992
11	St Paul's P.H.C.	Ashamena, Buruku LG	1983
12	St Agnes' P.H.C.	Yande, Kwande LG	1986
13	St Paul's P.H.C.	Sambe, Vandeikya LG	2003
14	St Theresa's P.H.C.	Mbangough, Kwande LG	2002
15	St Francis' P.H.C.	Hiitom, Kwande LG	1988
16	St Mary's P.H.C.	Alumuku, Ushongo LG	1989
17	St Monica's P.H.C.	Atimenya, Ushongo LG	1992
18	St Augustine's P.H.C.	Tauranga, Ushongo LG	1989
19	St Theresa's P.H.C.	Jorbua, Kwande LG	1987
20	Holy Trinity P.H.C.	Dagba, Kwande LG	2014
21	St Simon's P.H.C.	Javer, Kwande LG	2012
22	P.H.C. Dagba Mbaduku	Dagba Mbaduku, Vandeikya LG	2012

23	St Jacintha's P.H.C.	Utange, Ushongo LG	2006
24	St Paul's P.H.C.	Ikyaator, Vandeikya LG	2008
25	St Felix P.H.C.	Koti-yough, Vandeikya LG	2007
26	St Robert's P.H.C.	Adamgbe, Vandeikya LG	2019

Facilities under G.D.H.C.I. in Gboko Diocese.[19]

The primary healthcare centers are located at the grassroots, and they take care of minor illnesses. The importance of primary health care cannot be overemphasized. Their services are vital, and they cover a large number of the populace in the three (3) dioceses and the state. The populace living within and around these communities enjoy regular hospital, primary health care, and maternity services in the areas of health education, HIV/AIDS awareness and treatment, maternal and childcare, essential drugs, and food and water supply, treatment of minor ailments and dental care, mental health, and domestic accident prevention, prevention and treatment of endemic disease, and environmental and occupational health.

These health care centers/clinics/dispensaries are responsible for providing the primary health care needs of thc populacc. Most importantly, they partner with the ministry of health and donor agencies to eradicate the five killer diseases in children through immunisations and vaccinations. These centers havc bccn uscd in the forefront on the vaccination of polio, measles, yellow fever, and other programs such as distribution of mosquito nets, H.I.V. Testing and Counseling (H.T.C.) with sanitary health and hygiene information and awareness. All these have contributed immensely towards alleviating the health challenges of the populace.

[19] G.D.H.C.I. Secretariat (Unpublished Documents).

Apart from caring for the sick, the Catholic Church also undertakes capacity building for its staff across the three Dioceses. There is periodic training and workshop for health workers. This strengthens the Catholic healthcare system and brings the system operators up to speed with current trends. These workshops are also sometimes extended to people outside the scope of the Church's employment. Apart from these sessions, the Catholic Diocese of Gboko has established the School of Basic Medical Attendants. This category of health workers serves as clinical assistants at various health facilities and is doing very well. In all of its outreach, the Catholic Church in Tivland aims at providing a holistic medical approach, ranging from prevention to treatment to referral and health capacity-building.

The Church's Challenges in Healthcare Delivery in Tivland

A significant challenge faced by the Church in healthcare provision is the reconciliation of quality health care acquisition with the disbursement of same. Public health studies, the Millennium Development Goals, Sustainable Development Goals, as well as political economic studies are all in agreement today that the complex factors of population, income, and urbanisation, all have implications on healthcare. The more a nation spends on healthcare, the healthier its citizens will be. However, it is a reality that developing countries like Nigeria, (of which Tivland is a part) by nature can only afford minimum allocations to the health sector. Thus, quality healthcare becomes a commodity available only to the rich. In a society where specialised medicine is non-existent, and people have to pay heavily to sustain a healthy life but cannot afford it, adds to the complexity. This has made it very difficult for the Catholic healthcare system to maintain a high quality of care for the sick because every measure to improve health care makes it more expensive, reflecting the cost of care for the patient.

Other challenges would include a shortage of qualified staff, especially those who practice the Catholic faith and share the faith's views, doctrines, and teachings. Funding is also a significant challenge as medical supplies are very expensive, making it quite challenging to equip the health facilities with state-of-the-art facilities and equipment. Leadership is yet another encumbrance. Many a time, the leadership of these health facilities has to be imported. In as much as this could be a plus, it can at the same time be disadvantageous to the system as sometimes ownership is not seen in imported leadership.

Concluding Observation

It is evident that the Catholic Church holds an ace in healthcare provision in Tivland. Over the years, the standard has been maintained, and much progress has been made from the first missionary entry of health care in the land. We now have more hospitals, more clinics, and more P.H.C.s. However, healthcare must get to the point of a basic human need within the reach of the common man instead of a reserve commodity for those who can afford. Indeed, Constitution of the Federal Republic of Nigeria indicates that the government has the primary responsibility of providing healthcare to its citizens. Thus, it is indeed the duty of the government to support the health facilities for faith-based groups like the Catholic Church, who stand in the gap of government's failure in healthcare provision. It is part of government's legitimate duties.

Indeed, the laudable achievements of the Catholic Church in healthcare delivery notwithstanding, there is room for improvement. The Church will need to up its game in poverty reduction among its members to be able to access healthcare. Besides, consistent efforts to woo donors, implementing partners (IPs), philanthropists, and organisations to support the Church's health institutions should be prioritised. Finally, a standardised monitoring system should work for efficient supervision of our facilities, especially those in the rural areas, to ensure that they live up to expectations and maintain the standard.

Chapter Six

Catholic Social Thought, Political Participation, and Integral Human Development in Tivland

Remigius T. Ihula & Mike Utsaha[1]

Introduction

The presence of the Roman Catholic Church in the Benue valley has been phenomenal. From its humble beginnings as the prefecture of Otukpo in 1966, which later moved to Makurdi by 1968, there are today four dioceses out of the old Makurdi Diocese. An essential strategy towards the spiritual care of souls and the proclamation of the Gospel in Tivland by the Catholic Church has been interventions in the socio-cultural and political development of the area. Indeed, at present, Tivland owes its educational and social development mainly to the efforts of the Christian missionaries.

The social mission of the Church has a rich history, dating back to apostolic times with the institution of the *Diakonia* (Acts: 6:1-6). The theology and the flourishing of the social mission as we know it today is a direct outcome of the Vatican II documents on ecclesiology and the subsequent papal, synodal, and episcopal

1 Fr Remigius T. Ihula, a priest of Makurdi Diocese, is the Coordinator, Justice, Peace, and Development Foundation of the Diocese. Mike Utsaha, a legal practitioner, is the Executive Secretary, Resource & Planning Commission, Catholic Diocese of Makurdi.

statements that have followed that event. Today, this Gospel no longer focuses on the grievance about widows but emphasises the clear paths a society must follow to promote the "common good."

From the Enlightenment – through the Protestant Reformation, to the political revolutions which led to a secularised state, the advent of modernism up to the Second Vatican Council – the social doctrine of the Catholic Church continues to develop, with implications for all local Churches, including Tivland. Looking over the presence of the Catholic Church among the Tiv for a hundred years now, the Church necessarily has to ask where is it coming from, as it looks to the future. This question is vital for a church that seeks to add value to the integral development of its society.

Understanding the Concept of Catholic Social Thought

The Catholic social thought is a discernible body of teachings on the social order in its economic and political dimensions, emphasising the social nature of the human person, particularly the role of socialisation in human development.[2] Its foundations were laid by Pope Leo XIII's encyclical letter in 1891, which advocated economic distribution. The roots of the teaching are traced to the writings of Catholic theologians such as Saint Thomas Aquinas and Saint Augustine of Hippo derived from the concepts presented in the Holy Bible.[3]

The goal of Catholic social thought is to help Christians and people of goodwill to make better moral decisions and to shape values. When our values and morals as beings are shaped, it aids

[2] Richard Mc Brain, *Catholicism.* (Great Britain: Geoffrey and Chapman Publishers, 1981).

[3] *Pope Leo XIII Condemns Modern Philosophy.* http://skepticism.org/timeline/august-history/7929-pope-leo-xiii-condemns-modern-philosophy.html Accessed on August 4, 2021.

in understanding and alleviating economic and social problems to enable Christians to live in conformity with the values of the Gospels.[4] The Catholic Church has enumerated certain principles that are necessary to ensure that human dignity is respected and the common good promoted, which are termed the principles of the Catholic social thought, including: the dignity of the human person, the principle of participation, the common good, the universal destination of goods, and the preferential option for the poor.

In sum, the concept of Catholic social thought is distinctive in its consistent critiques of modern social and political ideologies such as liberalism, communism, anarchism; feminism, atheism, socialism, fascism, capitalism, and Nazism have all been condemned, at least in their pure forms, by several popes since the late nineteenth century.[5] Catholic social thought has always tried to find equilibrium between respect for human liberty, including the right to private property and subsidiary, and concern for the whole society, including the weakest and poorest.

The principles of Catholic social teaching revolve around the consistent ethic of life, which is anchored on the Catholic commitment to defend human life, from conception until natural death. The human person's right to life and dignity is the foundation of a moral vision for society. The Catechism of the Catholic Church explains:

> Those oppressed by poverty are the object of a preferential love by the Church, which since her origin and despite the failings of many of her members, has not ceased to work for their relief,

---

[4] Brigid Reynolds, *Values, Catholic Social Thought, and Public Policy*. (Dublin: CORI Justice, 2007).

[5] Catholic News Agency. *April 26 Teach-in on Catholic Social Teaching and NEPA.* https://www.catholicnewsagency.com/news/benedict-xvis-secretary-denies-rumors-that-he-is-close-to-death-11102 Accessed on August 1, 2021.

defense, and liberation through numerous works of charity, which remain indispensable always and everywhere *(no. 2448).*

From the earliest time to the development of sociological theory, social thought and social philosophy were the same. Social thought and sociological theory have a close relationship. Social thought progresses through wisdom, tales, theology, philosophy, rationalism, pragmatism, and scientific methods.

The Evolution Catholic Social Thought and its Application in Tivland

Catholic social thought has its roots in the messages of Hebrew prophets of the Old Testament. It fashioned the Church's response to historical conditions in Medieval and Early Modern Europe. The Church's approach to the early 19th-century revolutionary tide inaugurated by the French Revolution and Napoleonic era, through the Vatican II's inspiration from natural law were all steeped in the social doctrine. Indeed, the Catholic Church has since then, stepped up its social presence, assuming the moral responsibility for shaping values and institutions in the modern world, by proposing principles, values and directions that must guide just solutions.

Pope Paul VI stands out as the first Pontiff to devote an entire encyclical to the international development issue.[6] *Populorum Progressio* dwelt on the downside of development and the growing struggle between rich and developing nations. *Octagesimo Anno*[7] and *Rerum Novarum* pushed these arguments further. Pope John Paul II made the development issue and social justice a huge part of his teaching. Besides his encyclicals, *Sollicitudo Rei Socialis* (On Social Concerns) and *Centesimus Annus* John Paul II made

---

6 Paul VI, *Populorum Progressio* [Progress of Peoples] in 1967.

7 Paul VI, Call to Action in 1971.

it clear on his visit to Nigeria in February 1982 that Catholic laity should participate in politics.

Addressing the representatives of the Catholic Laity Council of Nigeria in Kaduna on February 14, 1982, John Paul II insisted that it is the special apostolate of the laity to bring Christian principles to bear upon the temporal order. According to him, such spheres of life as marriage and the family, trade and commerce, the arts and professions, politics and government, culture and national and international relations all need the touch of Christ through the presence of the laity.[8] The Catholic Bishops of Nigeria have consistently upheld this teaching in their numerous pastoral letters.

In Tivland, in the face of social revolution, industrialisation, and the spread of secularism, the Catholic Church employed the strategy of developing a robust and far-reaching role as a social service provider. Through its schools and hospitals, which have greatly flourished in the 21st century, the Church has improved access to quality and affordable health care services to rural populations, improved access to quality primary education for children in rural communities, created employment opportunities to youth, and enhanced community development in Tivland.

In the Old Makurdi Diocese, two names stood out as influencers of community engagement and development: Fr Patrick Foley CSSP and Fr Seamus Hunter CSSP. Foley was the pioneer coordinator of the Justice, Development, and Peace Commission in the Diocese. His basics of integral development works covered virtually all facets of life, from road culverts, and the construction of schools and health facilities all across the Diocese. Foley also ventured into agricultural development to introduce the populace

---

8 John Paul II, "Address to the Leaders of the Catholic Laity, Catechists and Christian Women of Nigeria," February 14, 1982, *L'Osservatore Romano*, (March-April, 1982, Vatican City), 15-16.

to improved agricultural practices for even economic purposes. To this day, the Agricultural Rural Training Center in Abwa still stands to his memory.

There were also the activities of Fr Seamus Hunter CSSP, who worked mainly in the rural parishes of Taraku, Naka, and later Agagbe. Hunter's development initiatives introduced the local populations to agricultural developments with the focus on promoting value-chain capabilities and transforming the attitudes of local farmers from subsistent farming to a more productive outlook. Like Foley on the other side of the old Makurdi Diocese, Hunter was profoundly involved in providing primary health facilities for the populations of his immediate pastoral assignment. He also provided minor construction activities like the building of culverts and access roads in the villages.

With their passing, the connections and opportunities that aided these two priests to carry out such physical developmental works were lost. However, the social development arms of the respective dioceses in Tivland have diversified into other areas requiring less monetary resources. The Makurdi Diocesan Foundation for Justice, Development, and Peace, for instance, with the help of donor agencies, has diversified its work to cover the following thematic areas: peacebuilding and conflict resolution, emergency response, protection /education services for Cameroonian Refugees in Benue and Akwa Ibom States, protection services for internally displaced persons in Benue State, good governance, human rights and legal aid, poverty reduction through promotion of microenterprise development, agricultural development.

The Dioceses of Gboko and Katsina-Ala are also engaged in handling internal displacement issues around Jato-Aka, Ikyogen, Anyiin, Zaki-Biam, Tor Donga and Awajir, since the situation affects almost 17 of the 23 Local Government Areas in Benue State. The Caritas Foundation for Justice and Peace in Gboko Diocese periodically undertakes voter-education campaigns, peace-building training and consultations with traditional rulers and youth across Tivland. Interventions in education for the IDPs and poverty reduction programs and agriculture development are key areas of engagement.

These social services delivered by the Catholic Church as an insight from the Catholic social thought have raised the overall standard of such services available to all irrespective diversity and religion. An example of the Catholic Church's commitment to shared human values in Tivland is the recent intervention that has transformed the Tiv practice of "befitting burial ceremonies" which were capital intensive. At the instance of the late Bishop Athanasius Usuh, the Catholic Church in Tivland issued pastoral guidelines on Church burials, encouraging burials to be done within ten (10) days of a person's passing and in simple graves. Christians of other denominations have widely adopted this practice, such as the NKST, and other churches in Tivland. This new development has significantly impacted rural communities in Tivland, which has helped install a culture of financial discipline during burial ceremonies.

Remarkably, however, the social involvement of the Catholic Church in Tivland did not extend to public service, viewing politics as incompatible with the practice of the Christian faith. The early missionaries to Africa were less concerned with the overall political process in any of the mission territories and, in particular, with the struggle for independence prevalent in some of the territories that were the target of evangelisation effort, including Tivland. The above, combined with the philosophy of separation of Church and state, accounts for the low level of Catholics participating in the political process.

Recent years have seen a remarkable improvement in this situation, and several factors account for this. The events preceding the Military takeover of power in 1966 and the outbreak of hostilities leading to the civil war engendered a certain level of consciousness for the relationship between power and politics and the interplay between the two, particularly in northern Nigeria. This has been adequately documented by Bishop Matthew Hassan Kukah in his celebrated book *Religion, Power, and Politics in Northern Nigeria* and requires no elaboration.

The consequent formation of the Christian Association of Nigeria (CAN), and, for the Catholic Church, in particular, the reorganisation of the Catholic Secretariat of Nigeria leading to the establishment of the Department of Church and Society, amongst others, provided a significant boost to the strategic program of raising consciousness in a much more formal and forward-looking manner to the issue of political participation of the Catholic Church in Nigeria generally.

Understandably, before the return in 1999 to civil and democratic rule, the Catholic Bishops Conference of Nigeria (CBCN) deployed more than one hundred thousand election observers to monitor the elections of that year, thus, providing a significant boost to this situation. Subsequent activities of the Justice Development and Peace Commissions (JDPC) of the respective dioceses of the Catholic Church in Nigeria, including all the dioceses in Tivland have continued to provide helpful impetus towards the progress that has been made.

Political Participation of Catholics in Tivland and Role of Catholic Bishops of Tivland

By 2006, and owing to the need for the Church to step up its role as a strategic partner in the peace process in Tivland, Bishop Athanasius Usuh introduced the 1st of January Prayer for Peace in Gboko, the seat of the Tor Tiv stool and headquarters of the Tiv people. As an offshoot of that initiative, in February 2015, the Catholic Bishops of Benue, in an unprecedented move, jointly signed a widely publicised document calling for peaceful campaigns and peaceful conduct of the general elections of that year. In a very formal sense, this would turn out to be the first time that all four Catholic Bishops of Benue will come together as one to issue and publicise a pastoral letter on a subject of common interest, encouraging Catholics to actively participate in politics as a means to bring the values of the Gospel into public service.

Although the Catholic Church in Tivland and elsewhere is decidedly apolitical, it is not the same thing as saying that the structures of the Church may not be adequately utilised towards the promotion of political participation in Tivland and Benue State at large. Thus, the Diocesan Catholic Laity Council of Nigeria (DCLCN), the Catholic Women Organisation (CWO), the Catholic Men Organisation (CMO), and the Catholic Youth Organisation of Nigeria (CYON) of the respective dioceses in Tivland have all been recent channels of sensitisation.

The Election of Fr Moses Adasu as Governor of Benue State

It is fair to say without any equivocation that the election of Rev. Fr Moses Adasu as Governor of Benue State in 1992 on the defunct Social Democratic Party (SDP) platform, is perhaps the greatest signpost yet to political participation of the Catholic Church in Tivland.

His emergence understandably elicited debate both within the Catholic Church and beyond on the fundamental question of whether it is permissible for Catholics to participate in politics. Although the answers to this fundamental question never really resulted in a groundswell of political consciousness on the part of the average Catholic in Tivland, the fact that the seeds had already been sown and they will germinate and bear fruits was only a matter of time.

Fr Moses Adasu ran against a fellow Catholic, Prof. Ignatius Ayua. Yet this did not form part of the more visible issues upon which the contest would be based, and this in itself is indicative of the shallow level of consciousness for sectional or sectarian affiliations in the political process in Tivland at the time.

This argument is supported and fortified by the fact that the Adasu – Ayua electoral contest fed into Nigeria's more significant political atmosphere. The contest for the office of president of Nigeria was between Chief MKO Abiola, candidate of the SDP, while Alhaji. Bashir Tofa, was the candidate of the National Republican Convention (NRC). Although Chief MKO Abiola was a well-known Muslim, it was immaterial to the voting public at the time that he picked a fellow Muslim Chief Babagana Kingibe as his running mate, and was widely acclaimed to be the winner of that election.

The Return to Democracy in 1999 and the Emergence of George Akume as Governor of Benue State

The circumstances leading to the establishment of an interim national government headed by Chief Ernest Shonekan and his subsequent removal from office and the emergence of Late General Sanni Abacha have already been well documented. Perhaps interesting here is the sudden death of Gen. Sani Abacha and the program of return to civil rule that was quickly put in place by his successor Gen. Abdulsalami Abubakar.

Under this program, a relatively unknown George Akume emerged as the People's Democratic Party's (PDP) candidate and was eventually elected governor in Benue State. Significantly, his wife, Chief Mrs Regina Akume, a devout Catholic of many years, effectively utilised her contacts and networks within the Church to launch a formidable campaign for the election of her husband into the office and his re-election in 2003 despite a relentless opposition by yet another Catholic Wantaregh Paul Iyorpuu Unongu of the All Nigeria Peoples Party (ANPP).

In our view, the campaign preceding the election of George Akume into office in 1999 is the first time that the question of faith background and denominational affiliation began to find its way into the political process in Tivland and the larger Benue state.

The Contest for the Stool of the Tor Tiv and the Emergence of Prof. James Ortese Ayatse

The contest for the office of Tor-Tiv is not a partisan political office, but it is nevertheless a political office that can feature conveniently in a conversation around political participation. This is mainly the case when the office is a creation of the political process, and the succession process also involves the actions of politically exposed persons.

In addition to several other planks upon which it was based, the entry of Sir Patrick Pillah, a devout and knighted Catholic, into the contest for Tor-Tiv, ran on the sentiment of a Catholic background. Catholic personages within and outside Benue threw their weight behind Sir Pillah and promoted his candidature based on his Catholic identity.

The the two topmost offices in the Executive branch of government at the time were occupied by non-Catholics. In light of the significant contributions of the Catholic Church to development in Tivland, the sentimental argument was that the office of Tor-Tiv should go to a Catholic. Although Sir Patrick Pillah lost out eventually, the seeds of sectional or sectarian consciousness had once again been sewn into the political process in Tivland and the larger Benue state.

Reverend Kyaan and the Contest for Governor of Benue State

The entry of Revd Frederick Kyaan, a pastor of the Universal Reformed Christian Church (URCC), also known as NKST Church, into the gubernatorial contest in 2019, ignited old hostilities and opened up new wounds. It equally raised, perhaps to the highest levels yet, sectional or sectarian political consciousness in Tivland.

Although he did not enjoy the overwhelming support of his church, he nevertheless was primarily perceived as a candidate with a religious identity. His supporters argued that since his church is one of the old generation churches much more like the Catholic Church, his candidacy should be prioritised over and above candidates who carry the identities of the new generation churches. Ortom would later win his re-election bid resoundingly trouncing Kyaan and the other contenders, but the fact remains that consciousness was beginning to build up gradually.

The Catholic Church and the Integral Development of Tivland

Thc Catholic Church is one of the foremost institutions credited for remarkable contributions to the development of Tivland and the larger Benue State. Since the creation of Makurdi Diocese and the subsequent dioceses, the Catholic faith has continued to grow among the Tiv. First was Otukpo Diocese in 1995, which Lafia quickly followed in 2001. In December 2012, the Tiv Catholic community was pleasantly surprised when Pope Benedict XVI created the dioceses of Gboko and Katsina in one fell swoop, thus bringing to three the number of Catholic dioceses in Tivland.

From a human resource perspective, the Church in Tivland has contributed significantly to the growth and development of the Catholic Church at universal, regional, and national levels. Before becoming Auxillary Bishop of Makurdi and later the first Bishop of Gboko, the then Fr William Avenya had provided service to the Regional Conference of Catholic Bishops of West Africa as Secretary General. While Fr Patrick Tor Alumuku served twelve years at the Africa section of the Vatican Radio in Rome, Fr Henry Akaabiam, is currently the Secretary General of the Symposium of Episcopal Conferences of Africa and Madagascar (SECAM), the African Continental Bishops Conference. The late Fr Alfred

Anongu Ashe was the first Tiv priest to serve at the Catholic Secretariat of Nigeria, followed by Fr Cornelius Akumba Azo.

Tiv Catholic clerics have also distinguished themselves in the academia. The late Fr James Shagba Moti successfully served two terms as Rector of the Catholic Institute of West Africa (CIWA) in Port Harcourt from 1997 to 2006. He had earlier served as Dean of the Faculty of Arts and later Head of Department at the Benue State University before his death. Fathers Moses Orhungur, Shagbaor F. Wegh, Vitalis Torwel, Didacus Kajo, Thomas Akpen, Kenneth Agede, Dominic Shimawua and a host of others have attained professorial ranks in their areas of academic concentration. Fr Peter Malu was the first Tiv priest to be commissioned as an officer in the Nigerian Army in 1982. In 2019, Fathers Philip Agber and Daniel Ude Asue were commissioned as officers in the USA Army, both in the rank of Captain, while Moses Ate was commissioned as Sub-Lieutenant in the Nigerian Navy. Other Tiv priests are also Chaplains in the Nigerian Army and the Nigerian Police Force.

Earlier, then Fr Athanasius Usuh served as the Chairman of the Benue State Football Association in 1984-1985, besides grooming young soccer talents in his darling team, the *Mosquitoes.* Usuh also served as Chairman of Christian Pilgrims Welfare Board. Fr Clement Akume Mato was famous for his radio program, *Iwanger*, which drew listeners across Tivland and beyond. The late Fr Christopher Ierwua Utov took over this program up to the 1990s. Today, the *Catholic Star Newspaper*, the *Starlive Radio*, and *Luminous Radio* are serving as voices of the people and alternatives to the rhetoric of government controlled media in Benue State and beyond. Equally, the Sisters of the Nativity and the Via Christi society, all indigenous congregations to Makurdi Diocese are making modest contributions to the propagation of the faith in Tivland.

The laity has equally contributed to the development of the Catholic faith in Tivland over the last one hundred years. Numerous dedicated Tiv Catholics have been honoured as Papal Knights and as awardees of various medals of honour. There is at the moment a thriving association of papal knights in Makurdi diocese headed by Mr Akor Ikpam. The Knighthood, particularly the Knights of Saint Mulumba (KSM) and the Knights of Saint John International (KSJI), all contribute to the faith's growth.

From the point of view of associations too, the Saint Augustine Tiv Catholic Community (SATCC) provides a platform for interaction for diaspora Tiv Catholics within and outside Nigeria. Remarkably, SATCC Abuja Archdiocese contributed financially and otherwise to installing the new Bishops in Gboko and Katsina-Ala and has continued to play host to them if and when they happen to be in Abuja. This particular activity is quite instructive since it underscores that we are learning from other Catholic Communities outside of Tivland and are even beginning to break new grounds in areas and activities that were not too common previously.

Other groups such as the Catholic Women Organisation (CWO), the Catholic Men Organisation (CMO), and the Catholic Youth Organisation of Nigeria (CYON) have contributed immensely to the process of deepening spirituality and the growth of the Catholic faith in Tivland over the years. The women group, in particular, have become so entrenched and influential in their activities that they become probably one of the most formidable and reliable lay groups in the Church in Tivland.

The role of the family in Tivland, and how some of the contributions they have made to the growth of the Catholic faith in Tivland also require some notice. It is, for instance, to the credit of the Late Michael Kinga Upaa of Nyiev in the present-day Guma Local Government, that one of the oldest parishes in the whole of northern Nigeria was established in Udei – the Sacred Heart Parish. Perhaps even more interestingly, the Upaa family has to its credit the uncommon trait of having produced two Catholic priests – the Late Fr Jude Upaa and Fr Tyolumun Upaa, SJ, and then a religious – Sr Esther Upaa. Also in this category belongs the Korayom Anyamhul family, which also has to its credit two priests – the Late Fr Felix Korayom and Fr Denis Korayom.

Admittedly, there is room for improvement in the extent to which we have fared as a worshipping community and as a people. Nevertheless, there is also the need to commend all those who, by their patience, resilience, hard work, personal sacrifices and unflinching commitment to the faith have brought about the significant growth we have witnessed over the years. The Church has established schools, hospitals, integrated farms and, more recently, is beginning to delve into the transportation business as we have seen in the Catholic Diocese of Katsina-Ala. We also note with great satisfaction the rich liturgy we continue to enjoy wholly in Tiv language.

Conclusion

While it is imperative to look to the positive developments associated with the Church in Tivland there is a bleak future ahead of us. Besides the massive flow of Catholics to Pentecostal churches, the Mass has become a platform for the celebration of politically exposed persons (PEPs), all in the guise of thanksgiving celebrations and an avenue to prioritise fundraising over and above matters of spirituality and deepening of the faith. The sanctity of the Holy Mass as a Eucharistic celebration and an opportunity for reconciliation with the Father of all humanity needs to be revisited urgently.

Relatedly, Bishop Usuh's *An Agenda for a Nation without an Agenda* can be a valuable tool for the Catholic Church in Tivland towards schooling younger Catholics in the social teaching of the Church. Catholic Church authorities in Tivland should employ this resource as a policy guide to encourage full participation of Catholics in the policy process in Tivland and Benue State. While the creation of additional dioceses is helpful in terms of bringing the faith closer to the people, there is need to create a synergy within the three Catholic dioceses of Tiv extraction.

Chapter Seven

The First Tiv Catholic Priests

Gabriel T. Wankar & Joseph Eneji[1]

Introduction

In Tivland, north-central Nigeria, the Catholic Church emerged from a humble beginning in the first two decades of the 20th century. Expatriate missionaries of the Holy Ghost Fathers opened up the frontiers of Benue valley. In 1961, the late James Akor became the first Diocesan Seminarian to complete form five at the Minor Seminary in Keffi, and in 1970, he made history becoming the first Tiv man to be ordained a Catholic priest, ten years after the creation of the old Makurdi Diocese.[2]

A year later, a more phenomenal number was recorded for the nascent Church in Tivland with the ordination of seven Tiv sons into the presbyterate of the Catholic Church. They were Athana-

---

1 Fr Gabriel T. Wankar (M.Sc. Development Studies, M. Th. Ecclesiology, S.T.L. Systematic Theology, PhD Systematic Theology) served as Director of Communications for the Catholic Diocese of Makurdi, and a secretary to the Benue State chapter of the Christian Association of Nigeria, (CAN). He is currently assigned in the Archdiocese of San Francisco, California. Joseph Eneji is an Adjunct Faculty, Institute of Humanities, Pan-Atlantic University, Lagos, and a doctoral candidate in the Department of History and Strategic Studies, University of Lagos, Akoka, Lagos.

2 Shagbaor F. Wegh, "The Emergence of the Catholic Diocese of Makurdi" in *Catholic Diocese of Makurdi at 50: A Celebration of Service to Humanity* Ed. Shagbaor F. Wegh (Makurdi: Selfer Academic Press Ltd., 2010), 32-33.

sius Atule Usuh, Benjamin Adzor, Dominic Vaachia Yuhe, Simon Kwaghtyo Iverver, Edward Hen Maaer, Stephen Tamkper Beba, and Moses Orshio Adasu. This marked a watershed in the annals of the Catholic Church in the area. Having these young men from a clime that did not know the priestly vocation hitherto was significant. At a critical time when change and continuity were at a melting point,[3] these young men embraced the new Christian faith and the vocations to the Catholic priesthood with commitment and resolve.

The ordination of these gentlemen as Catholic priests was timely and eventful when the Church's indigenisation was a front-burning issue in Nigeria and elsewhere in Africa. For the Catholic Church in Tivland, the retreat of the European missionaries from the field did not create a vacuum. Elsewhere within Nigeria the situation was the opposite, while in Tivland the seven priests filled the void.[4] They continued with the legacies of the white priests who planted the Catholic faith in the area. Indeed, among those ordained in 1971, the indigenous leadership of the Catholic Church in Tivland emerged. The set produced the first indigenous Catholic Bishop of Makurdi Diocese, Late Bishop Athanasius Usuh, who served from 1989 to 2016. Also, from among their ranks emerged the first Catholic Priest – Governor of a state in Nigeria, Reverend Father Moses Oshio Adasu. He was Governor of Benue state 1992-1993. It is apt to say the set produced trailblazers in various spheres of Tiv society.

---

3 William Shija, "Reverend Father Beba: The Oldest Catholic Priest in Benue is Dead," https://ng.opera.news/ng/en/religion/f647cc4b99d29bb6c74b6838c0370a94. Accessed August 7, 2021.

4 Joseph Ukpo, "Statistical Data of the Catholic Church in Nigeria," in *The History of The Catholic Church in Nigeria*, Eds. A. O. Makozi & G. J. Afolabi Ojo (Lagos: Macmillan Nigeria Publishers, 1982), 104.

Looking at their contribution to Tivland and society, one would appreciate their place in history as change agents. As trailblazers, they opened the door for the rest of the young men who later embraced the priestly vocation in Tivland. The vocation boom into the Catholic priesthood witnessed in Tivland today was signalled by this group of seven. During a celebration in 2016 in honour of Rev. Fr Stephen Beba (then alive), the Catholic Bishop of Makurdi Diocese, Most Reverend Wilfred Anagbe, acknowledged the untiring efforts of the first indigenous priests in Tivland in shaping the history of Christianity in Nigeria.

Indeed, their legacies are pretty monumental, given the Catholic Church's achievements in the area today. These transcend both the religious and secular spheres of Tiv society. No doubt, every Catholic priest of Tiv descent consider them to be the grandfathers of the indigenous Catholic priesthood in the Tiv ethnic group. Like the wise men of Bethlehem, they showed the way to this noble vocation. One way of celebrating this excellent pioneer team will be to record their biographies as a reference for future generations. This chapter is an attempt to chronicle the life stories of these seven trailblazers. Efforts will be made to present some topical aspects of their experiences and how they affected their society. This account relied extensively on oral interviews and a few documentary materials, employing the facility of interviews with knowledgeable informants who interacted directly or indirectly with these priests on different occasions while they were still alive.

Most Reverend Athanasius Atule Usuh

The Most Reverend Athanasius Atule Usuh was born to the late Pa Joseph Usuh Anachi and Mama Edna Hilemo Usuh of Mbatyough, Mbagen in Buruku Local Government Area of Benue

State on May 2, 1942.[5] He was the second born in a family of eleven siblings. The young Athanasius attended St Theresa's Primary School Abwa from 1951 to 1958, graduating as a pioneer set.[6] Shortly after finishing his primary education, he taught at RCM Abayol at Ukan in Ushongo local government area from 1959-1960. He was then transferred to RCM Kusuv in Mbatitiv, Yandev, where he taught for one year, 1960-1961. In 1961, Atule gained admission and studied at St James Junior Seminary Keffi (now Yandev). He finished his formative studies at the Minor seminary in 1965. While in the Junior Seminary, his talents in music and sports were evident as he was made the choirmaster and football captain of the school.

Again, leaving the junior seminary, the young Atule taught for a while at the then St Augustine's Teachers College Lafia in 1966. This demonstrates the passion he had for imparting knowledge to people. His desire to answer the call to the priesthood came to fruition with his admition to the famous Bigard Memorial Seminary Enugu in September 1966, but had to leave at the outbreak of the Nigerian civil war.[7] He became part of the group to start St. Augustine Major Seminary in Keffi, which was later moved to Jos.

It is worthy to note that, at the major seminary, the young seminarian Athanasius Usuh was an active football player and an avid choirmaster. Thus, his love and mastery of the round leather

---

5 Office of Communications, Catholic Diocese of Makurdi, *Memorial Journal for Most Reverend Athanasius Atule Usuh: Bishop Emeritus of Makurdi Diocese, 1942- 2016.* (Makurdi, 29th July, 2016), 2.

6 Ibid.

7 Office of Communications, Catholic Diocese of Makurdi, *Memorial Journal for Most Reverend Athanasius Atule Usuh*, 2.

game earned him the school captaincy from third-year until graduation.[8] In the same way, he was also the seminary's choirmaster and music teacher with the help of Sr Camel Dodd.[9] According to Rev. Fr Moses Iorapuu, "while in the major seminary, the young Athanasius was many things rolled into one."

Athanasius Usuh, along with his six colleagues, was ordained a Catholic priest on December 19, 1971. Since this group were ordained in their third year of theology, they had to go back to the seminary immediately following ordination to complete their studies in 1972. Upon graduation, Fr Usuh was assigned to St Patrick's Parish Taraku in January 1973, where he founded a soccer team, *The Mosquitoes*, a team of under-13 boys who could truly sting with their skills. Professor Joseph Tor Iorapuu was a goalkeeper of *The Mosquitoes*. Fr Usuh was moved to Sacred Heart Parish, Udei, in December 1974, and served till December 1975.

Aside from pastoral assignments, Fr Usuh had stints in the academic environments too. For instance, in January 1976, he was called to take up a new challenge: his Bishop (Bishop Murray) seconded him to the St Augustine Major Seminary Jos.[10] While at St Augustine seminary he was made dean of formation and director of music, in addition to academic engagements. At the same time he was also appointed the Diocesan Vocations' Director of his home diocese. He spent two and half years in the seminary and was subsequently sent to the United States of America to study at the Catholic University, Washington DC. He studied liturgical

8 Ibid.

9 Ibid, 3.

10 Ibid, 4.

music and returned to the diocese in 1980. On his return to Nigeria, Fr Atule Usuh was appointed Rector of St James' Minor Seminary, Makurdi, where he stayed for five years.[11] His responsibility as Rector was preparing students who would be trained as future priests for the diocese.

The Benue State Government utilised his passion for soccer and organisational skills by appointing him Chairman of the State Football Association from 1984 to 1985. Gate takings at the stadia rose by 300% within that year. Fr Athanasius also served the state as Chairman, Benue State Christian Pilgrims Welfare Board after the expiration of Bishop Achigili of the Methodist Church. In 1986 he was appointed Parish Priest of Holy Ghost Parish, Makurdi, and Vicar General of Makurdi Diocese. He was appointed co-adjutor Bishop of Makurdi Diocese and consecrated on January 6th 1988, by Pope John Paul II in Rome. He was installed on October 21, 1989, at the IBB Square as the first indigenous Catholic Bishop of Makurdi Diocese. Until his death, Bishop Athanasius was the third Catholic Bishop of Makurdi Diocese.

Bishop Usuh chose his motto: *Ter Mkuma Ga*, a Tiv phrase that loosely translates as "Lord I am not worthy." He implies that the saying captured the circumstances that led him to become bishop and the challenges ahead. It was also a sign of deep humility for the honour given him to serve as bishop.[12] He further adds that he felt he was not the most intelligent of his mates, yet God found him worthy to be the Bishop. With this, he submitted in humility to the will of God in his life.

As the first indigenous Bishop of the old Makurdi diocese, Athanasius Usuh recorded phenomenal achievements. These cuts across education, health care, spiritual, and vocations into the

---

[11] Ibid, 5.

[12] Ibid, 5.

priesthood. In the creation of dioceses, under his bishopric, the mother diocese of Makurdi birthed Otukpo, Lafia, and recently, the contemporary duo of Gboko and Katsina-Ala. The creation of these dioceses under his apostolic domain was occasioned by the constant increase in Catholic faithful in the area. Alongside these feats, Bishop Usuh was also instrumental in the ordination and installation of bishops in the respective dioceses.

Thus, his reign saw to the likes of Late Bishop Fidelis Ogah of Otukpo, Bishop (now Archbishop) Matthew Ishaya Audu of Lafia,[13] Bishop Michael Apochi of Otukpo, Bishop William Avenya of Gboko, Late Bishop Peter Adoboh of Katsina-Ala, and lastly, Bishop Wilfred Anagbe of Makurdi diocese. Usuh resigned as Bishop of Makurdi on March 28, 2015 upon failing health, and died on July 14, 2016. He was laid to rest at the Cathederal Church of Our Lady of Perpetual Help, Makurdi, on July 29, 2016.

Reverend Father Dominic Vaachia Yuhe, PhD

Dominic Vaachia Yuhe was born into the family of Mr. John Yuhe Mtswen Gbaka and Mrs Anna Kwagher Yuheat Ihugh in Vandeikya Local Government Area of Benue State around 1946. He attended St Augustine (now St Winifred) Catholic primary school Ihugh from 1953-1957, St Joseph's Korinya in 1958, and completed primary education at St Theresa's Naka in 1959-1960. Dominic was admitted into St James' Seminary, Keffi, in 1961, where he obtained the London University GCE in 1965.

His training for the priesthood began in 1966 at the Bigard Memorial Seminary, Enugu alongside Athanasius Usuh. He was, however, forced to leave Enugu because of the Nigerian civil war. The

[13] Until his installation as the Archbishop of Jos Archdiocese, Most Rev. Mathew Ishaya Audu was formerly the Bishop Catholic diocese of Lafia.

young Dominic further joined the pioneer set of the newly established St. Augustine's Major Seminary, Keffi, (now in Jos). At the Seminary, he was at various times, the Head of the Food Committee, the first Editor of the *Awakening Light Magazine*, President of the Debating Society, Assistant Auxiliary, and First Auxiliary. Dom Yuhe was a skilled soccer player on the seminary team, and his fans referred to him as "404." He was finally ordained a Catholic priest on December 19, 1971, at St John's Catholic Church, Gboko.

Following ordination, Fr Yuhe served as an assistant Priest at St. John's Parish, Gboko, from January, 1973 – August, 1974. In September 1974, he proceeded to Rome for higher studies. He completed his studies in Rome in 1978, where he obtained the Ph.D. (Moral Theology) at the Pontifical University of St Thomas Aquinas. Similarly, he obtained a Bachelor of Arts in Philosophy and a Masters in Theology at the same University.

On his return to the diocese, Fr Dominic Yuhe was engaged in the teaching apostolate. He worked as a lecturer at Murtala College of Arts, Science, and Technology, Makurdi, now Benue State Polytechnic, Ugbokolo (1979-1982). From 1982-1993 he served as Senior and Principal Lecturer at the School of Basic Studies, Makurdi, and rose to be Head of the Department of Arts.

In 1989 Fr. Yuhe was appointed Parish Priest of St Theresa's Parish, High Level, Makurdi, and in the same year appointed Vicar-General of Makurdi Diocese – the post he held till death in 1998.

Reverend Father Simon K. A. Ivever

Simon Kwaghtyo Anyom Ivever was born around 1944 to Peter Ivever Igbe and Martha Maalu in Mbagen, Buruku Local Government Area of Benue State. After his primary education, he enrolled at St. James' Minor Seminary, Keffi, (now Yandev),) in 1957. He graduated from the Minor Seminary in December 1962. However, he would not start studies at the Major Seminary until

1963 due to the change of the academic year at Bigard Memorial Seminary, Enugu. At Enugu, he studied Philosophy for three years.

In July 1966, he completed his studies in philosophy. Again, he was not able to begin the study of Theology because of the Nigerian Civil War. He was then sent to teach at the Minor Seminary in Keffi, where he spent one and a half years. It is interesting to note that the year he started teaching at Keffi, the group he would eventually be ordained with started their studies in Philosophy in Keffi. This was the birth of what is now St Augustine's Major Seminary, Jos.

In 1968 Simon Ivever returned to the Major Seminary to study Theology–the last step towards priestly ordination–but this time at SS Peter and Paul Major Seminary, Bodija, Ibadan. Simon was ordained a priest for the Catholic Diocese of Makurdi by His Lordship, Bishop Donald Murray CSSP (second Bishop of Makurdi Diocese) in the Church at St. John, Gboko on December 19, 1971.

With his priestly ordination, Fr Simon worked in the following parishes: St Patrick's Parish, Taraku, 1972; St Ann's Adikpo, January – July 1973; Sacred Heart, Udei, July to December, 1973; Christ the King, Vandeikya, December 1973 to October 1978; St. John's Parish, Gboko 1978 to 1995; St Joseph the Worker, Anongo Tyowanye from 1995 to May 28, 1998 when he died.

Monsignor Stephen Tamkper Beba

Born on October 20, 1945, in Gwer-West Local Government Area of Benue State, Stephen Beba enrolled at St James' Junior Seminary, Keffi, in 1962. He completed his studies at the seminary in 1966 with the London University GCE. Consequently, in 1967 Stephen entered the newly established St Augustine Major Seminary, Jos, to study for the priesthood. He was finally ordained on December 19, 1971, at Gboko.

As a priest, he served on various vital committees in Makurdi Diocese and worked in these parishes: St Ann's Adikpo, three months in 1972; St Joseph's Korinya, 1973 – 1976; St Stephen's Lessel, 1976 – 1978; Holy Ghost Makurdi, 1978 – 1980; Holy Ghost, 1982 – 1986, Christ the King, Vandeikya; St John's Parish, Gboko; and lastly, St Mary's Parish, North-Bank, Makurdi. Fr Beba had a masters' degree in psychology from York University, Toronto, and another masters' degree in Canon Law St Paul University, Ottawa.

On October 29, 2019, Fr Stephen Beba was elevated to the position of Monsignor within the Catholic Church, naming him as a Chaplain of Holiness.[14] Thus, Fr Stephen Beba became the first priest of the diocese to be honoured with the title of Monsignor since the creation of the Makurdi diocese on April 2, 1959[15] Monsignor Stephen Beba died on Thursday, February 4, 2021, at age 76. Among the class of 1971, Monsignor Stephen Beba was the last to pass on to the great beyond.

Reverend Father Benjamin A. Adzor, PhD

Benjamin Adzor was born in a small village in Mbakyan-Ugee in the Njiriv District of Gwer Local Government Area of Benue State in Makurdi Diocese in 1945. Benjamin was the firstborn of his parents in a family of six siblings – three brothers and two sisters. Regrettably, his father, Adzor Uga, died when Benjamin was very young. His widow mother, Martha, shouldered the family's responsibilities. The young Benjamin attended St Martin's Catholic Primary School, Abenga, from 1955 – 1958. He then proceeded to Awajir Catholic Senior Primary School, where he studied from

[14] "Nigeria's Reverend Father Stephen Beba made a Chaplain of Holiness by Pope Francis," https://www.nigerianwatch.com/nigerias-reverend-father-stephen-beba-made-a-chaplain-of-his-holiness-by-pope-francis/. Accessed on September 6, 2021.

[15] Including the other dioceses that were created from the old Makurdi diocese.

1959 – 1961. Here, he obtained his First School Leaving Certificate (FSLC). In 1962 he was admitted into St James' Junior Seminary, Keffi where he started his priestly training. He completed his Junior Seminary Studies in 1966.

In 1967 St Augustine's Major Seminary Jos was opened for Northern Dioceses with temporary quarters in Keffi. In the same year, he was accepted into St Augustine's Major Seminary to study Philosophy and Theology. Benjamin Adzor was ordained a priest on December 19, 1971, at St John's Catholic Parish Gboko with six others by His Lordship, Bishop Donald Murray, Catholic Bishop of Makurdi Diocese.

In 1973, Rev. Fr Benjamin Adzor was assigned to St Mary's Parish, Wukari, as Assistant Priest. In 1976 the Bishop of Makurdi Diocese, Most Rev. Murray decided to send him to Rome for further studies. He studied Dogmatic Theology at the Pontifical Urban University, Rome, obtaining a Ph.D. in 1978.

On his return to Nigeria from further studies, Fr Benjamin Adzor was sent to St Augustine's Major Seminary, Jos, to teach Dogmatic Theology. He left the Major Seminary by the end of May 1980 to undertake Parish work. Dr Adzor worked in many Parishes within the old Makurdi Diocese, including Christ the King, Vandeikya; St Gabriel, Namor; Gboko-West, and finally in residence at St Mary's Parish North-Bank Makurdi till his death in 2010.

H. E. Reverend Father Moses Orshio Adasu

Moses Adasu was born on June 12, 1945. He attended St Pius Primary School, Awajir, where he completed his primary education in 1961. He proceeded to St James' Junior Seminary, Keffi (1962 – 1965) and St Augustine Major Seminary, Jos (1967 – 1972), an affiliate of the Propaganda Fide, 1969 – 1972, graduating with a bachelor's degree in Divinity. On December 19, 1971, Fr Adasu was ordained a Catholic priest of the Catholic Diocese of Makurdi along with six others. He returned to the Seminary to complete his studies along with his colleagues, since they were ordained priests in third year theology. After his ordination, Fr Adasu took up a teaching appointment with Government Teachers College, Jos, Plateau State.[16] Next, he served as a Curate, St Mary's Parish, Otukpo, in 1974, before proceeding to St Johns University, New York City 1975 – 1976, earning a Master of Arts degree, and then at the Catholic University of America, DC 1976 – 1978, where he gained a Masters of religious education. While studying, he also worked at St Mary's Rectory, New York, from 1975 – 1976.

Upon his return, Father Adasu was assigned as Parish Priest of Holy Ghost Parish Makurdi Between 1980 and 1986. He also took up an appointment as an Assistant Lecturer at the Advanced Teachers College, Akwanga (Now COE), Nasarawa State, where his courses included Political and Developmental issues. He later transferred his services to College of Education (COE), Katsina-Ala, where he rose through the ranks to become Senior Principal Lecturer, and Dean of School of Arts.[17] While at COE Katsina-Ala, Adasu was elected to the Constituent Assembly with the approval of the Catholic Church in 1988, where he worked on the 1989 Constitution as a technocrat. Chaired by Honorable Justice Anthony Aniagulu, the Benue team to the Constituent Assembly included Adasu alongside Dr J. Ortyoyande, Pastor Moses A. Antse, Orbunde Gbim Gbande, Ehnr. Yakubu Agada, and Professor David Iornem.

Between 1984 and 1990, he was Chairman, Presbyteral Council of the Catholic Diocese of Makurdi, and a member of the

[16] Cf. Terhemba Wuam, *Moses Orshio Adasu: Religion, Politics and Development.* (Makurdi: Aboki Publishers, 2004).

[17] Ibid.

college of Consulters. In addition, he was Dean, Makurdi Deanery, and at a time Vicar-General of the Diocese. Other responsibilities included, member, Christian Pilgrim's Welfare Board; member, Benue State Council on Prerogative of Mercy and the Advisory Council, Episcopal Commission on Africa; Member, Board of the College of Education, Katsina-Ala.[18]

Adasu ventured into partisan politics on the platform of the SDP, where he ran in the Benue State gubernatorial elections in 1991 and defeated Mr Ignatius Ayua of the National Republican Convention (NRC).[19] Consequently, he was elected the second Executive Governor of Benue State from January 1992 to November 1993. Regrettably, the military interrupted the administration, and Fr Adasu returned to the pulpit as a Catholic priest where he served at Ikyogen and Adikpo. Later in 2000, he was appointed Commissioner, Independent Corrupt Practices and Other Related Offences Commission (ICPC), where he had a brief stint. He returned into full partisan politics on the platform of Alliance for Democracy (AD) in 2003.[20]

Within the short period his administration lasted, his achievements were phenomenal. He founded Benue State University, Makurdi, in 1992. He reactivated and upgraded the College of Education, Oju. He conceived the concept of the Tarka Foundation, named after Senator Joseph Sarwuan Tarka, and launched it on July 2, 1992.[21] He started other projects, including Abinsi Roofing Tiles Company and the Katsina-Ala fruit Juice Company.

As a member of the Alliance for Democracy (AD) party, he challenged the then incumbent Governor George Akume of the

---

18 Ibid.

19 Ibid.

20 Ibid.

21 Ibid.

Peoples' Democratic Party PDP in the April 2003 gubernatorial elections. He was not successful. In September 2004, he was head of one of the National Convention Committees for the AD, after a factional split in the party caused by the return of former chairman Ahmed Abdulkadir.

Regrettably, on November 20, 2005, Fr Adasu died at a private hospital in Lagos during a brief illness. He was buried at the cemetery of Catholic priests at Our Lady of Perpetual Help Cathedral, Makurdi Diocese. After his death, Benue State University conferred an honourary doctorate on Adasu

Reverend Father Edward Hen Maaer

Edward Maaer was born on February 10, 1945, at Police Barracks Gboko. He hailed from Ukan in the present-day Ushongo Local Government Area of Benue state. He started his elementary school at St John Roman Catholic Mission School, Gboko, and proceeded to St James' Seminary Keffi in 1961, alongside Stephen Beba, Moses Adasu, and Benjamin Adzor. Upon graduation from the Minor Seminary, he was admitted to St Augustine Major Seminary, Jos (1967 – 1972), an affiliate of the Propaganda Fide, graduating with a bachelor's degree in Divinity.

On December 19, 1971, Fr Maaer was ordained a Catholic priest of the Catholic Diocese of Makurdi along with six others. He was first assigned to Christ the King Parish, Vandeikya, and later St Margaret's Tor-Donga. He was appointed Parish Priest of St Anthony's Parish, Zaki-Biam, where his ill-health manifested. He left Zaki-Biam in March 1976 to seek medical attention outside the country and was replaced by Fr Moses Orhungur on April 9, 1976. While in Kano to make his medical trip abroad, the medical team responsible for managing his condition advised against his making the journey, indicating that his condition would not allow him make the air travel successfully. Fr Maaer then returned to the diocese, and was sent to St Anns Adikpo, where he stayed for a few months and later died.

Since he was the first to die out of the seven, and the Diocese at the time had no cemetery, he was buried at the present St John's Cathedral in Gboko, where his grave can be found by the side of the Church leading to the Sisters convent. An added reason for his burial site is said to have been a result of a disagreement between Yandev and Ukan people, regarding Fr Maaer's progeny.

Chapter Eight

The Unique Story of the Catholic Faith in the Sankara Axis

Godwin Bagu & Moses Igba[1]

Introduction

The Sankara axis of the Catholic Church in Tivland came under the evangelising activities of the German Holy Ghost Fathers from Gboko. Fr Strick, who was in charge of the newly opened Roman Catholic mission in Gboko, crossed river Katsina-Ala and traveled to Chonku, a village settlement between Jootar (in Benue State) and Wukari (in Taraba State) which were then in Muri Province. There he baptised five infants and celebrated the first Holy Mass for the Wukari Community on May 5, 1938. This Mass was attended predominantly by a handful of Catholics of Cameroonian and Igbo extraction[2]

Counting on the gains of the Mass and infant baptism, the Prefecture of Benue applied for and acquired land which in the same year, 1938, established St Mary's Mission, now St Mary's

---

1 Fr Godwin Bagu is the Vicar General of the Catholic Diocese of Katsina Ala, and Professor Emeritus of St Thomas Aquinas' Major Seminary Makurdi. Fr Moses Igba, a priest of Katsina Ala Diocese, is the administrator of the Cathedral Church of St Gerald Majella in Katsina-Ala.

2 Nsima Justin Ekong, *History of St Mary Catholic Church, Wukari, Taraba State* (Wukari, 2020), 3.

Parish, Wukari. This mission then took over from St John's Mission, Gboko, the task of evangelising the entire territory of Sankara – a remarkable achievement after the failure of the mission founded by Pere Leon Lejeune at Ibi on September 6, 1902.

This was achieved through the "Munshi Mission at Ogoja" led by Pere Jules Douvry on March 15, 1921, as narrated to Pere Lena by the latter, that within two months of travel among the Tiv, he managed to talk to all the Chiefs in Katsina-Ala division. They promised to send their children to school. His enthusiasm, capturing his evangelising zeal for the territory, is further expressed in this letter: "even more amazing, several of them have refused the Protestants of the Dutch Reformed Church Mission. These have been in Katsina-Ala division for seven years, but they have hardly made any progress; the reason been that up to last August, most of this country was still closed to Europeans."[3]

With the Second World War outbreak, the English and Irish province of the Holy Ghost Fathers (Spiritans) took charge of the Pastoral activities at St Mary's Mission Wukari. Fathers Doolin and O'Toole, who led this effort, were stationed in Gboko. Eventually, in 1945, Fr Bert Maher built a presbytery for the parish. The evangelising activity from subsequent priests of this parish started new mission stations like Angov, Nenshi, Akaa in 1950, and many others to follow.

In 1965, the people of Zaki-Biam, through the influence of Magaret Haalakpa Bako (a converted prostitute), and Catechist Emmanuel Mnzuulga Agede, had contact with the Catholic Church at St John Akaa, a settlement near Kyado and brought it to Zaki-Biam where the mission was established at its temporal site, a

---

3 *Annales Apostolique*, July-August, 1921, 102. (Mutilated pages found in the archives at St Joseph's Parish, Korinya).

place then called *Kenti*, beniseed Market.[4] In 1966 the mission was moved to its permanent site. Fr J. Carrol CSsp was mandated to make all the proper arrangements to establish St Anthony's Parish, Zaki-Bam, and St Margaret Parish, Tor-Donga as independent missions from St. Mary's Parish, Wukari. Zaki-Biam was created as a parish on January 6, 1967, with Fr Gerald Avery CSSp appointed as the first parish priest. St Magaret Tor-Donga was next in the same year after Mr Kwaghlaade Tor-Injiov, who was the Church Committee Chairman, opposed the construction of the Presbytery at Angov where the mission was founded originally with an established primary school.

St Anthony's Parish Zaki-Biam in 1972 gave birth to All Saints Parish, Tsenge-Ugba and St Margaret Tor-Donga did the same with the creation of St Gerard Majella, a mission station established in 1957 in Katsina-Ala elevated to a parish on September 9, 1971. Fr Gerard Avery was appointed the first parish priest.

With the creation of more parishes out of these initial two, in 1984, the whole of Sankara territory was granted the dicta of a deanery with the name Katsina-Ala and Katsina-Ala as the seat. As more churches sprang up with more parishes and pastoral areas, in 1999, the deanery of Zaki-Biam was created for easier ecclesiastical administration, making two deaneries in the territory. On December 29, 2012, the Holy Father, Pope Benedict XVI, at the request of Most Rev. Athanasius A. Usuh, Bishop of Makurdi Diocese, created the Katsina-Ala diocese out of Makurdi diocese, with full ecclesiastical rights. Msgr Peter Iornzuul Adoboh was appointed as the first bishop and was ordained and installed on February 23, 2013. He died on February 14, 2020, nine days before his seventh episcopal ordination anniversary.

---

4 Moses A Igba in an oral interview with John Ugboho and elders of St Anthony's Parish, Zaki-Biam, May 19, 2016.

Consequently, Pope Francis appointed Most Rev. William A. Avenya, the Bishop of Gboko Diocese, as the apostolic administrator *sede vacante* of Katsina-Ala diocese on February 15, 2020. The diocese covers the following Local Government Areas of Benue State: Katsina-Ala Local Government Area, Ukum Local Government Area, Logo Local Government Area, part of Buruku Local Government Area, and Guma Local Government Area. The diocese stretches into part of the Awe Local Government Area of Nasarawa State, with an area of about 6, 465 km^2 and a population of about 444, 680 Catholics out of about 1,152,700 persons in the area. [5] This essay joins the conversation on the hundred years of the Catholic Church from the angle of presenting prevailing security challenges in Sankara and the efforts of the Catholic Church in mediating and preventing these conflicts, suggesting what can be done to restore peace going forward.

Insecurity in Katsina-Ala Diocese

In the good olden days, people, particularly Tiv from other areas of Tivland, generally referred to as *Kparev,* came in large numbers to settle in different parts of *Sankara*, generally because of its peaceful nature in order to farm. Civil servants virtually turned into farmers, going into the villages for farming activities because of the area's fertility. Other tribes too came for commercial purposes, mainly because of the abundant and cheap food items. If Benue State could be described as "The Food Basket" of Nigeria, it is *Sankara* that the food primarily comes from.[6] These were possible because of the peace that prevailed in *Sankara*. One can recall that

---

5 Catholic Diocese of Katsina-Ala, *Quinquennium Report* (2019, 2).

6 Wilfred Atser, "Effects of Insecurity and Lack of Peace in Sankara Axis and Katsina-Ala Diocese." (Unpublished symposium paper marking one year memorial of the death of Bishop Peter Adoboh, 2021), 1.

when Kogi State was created out of Benue state in 1991, many Igalas who were living in Katsina-Ala were not ready transfer their services to the newly created state in Igalaland. For example, many Igalas working at the College of Education, Katsina-Ala in Benue State, were compelled to leave when their files were unilaterally taken to Lokoja, the Kogi State capital.[7]

However, with time, some skirmishes developed among the people of *Sankara* themselves: between Shitile and Ikyurav, Shitile and Ukum, the people of *Sankara* and *Kparev*. This was mainly a result of land disputes. The Tiv are agrarian, and with population explosion, there is bound to be a scramble for limited land. This has usually resulted in land disputes and crises.

Secondly, Sankara geopolitical axis borders Taraba and Nassarawa States. Such composition has occasioned historical inter-tribal wars between Tiv-Jukun, Tiv-Fulani, to Tiv-Kuteb, to mention but a few. Thus, the Tiv of Sankara extraction has over time improved on their preparedness to meet external adversaries. It is this consciousness that has informed the long succession of militia kingpins.[8] However, with the return of democracy in 1999, politicians started campaigns, and there were pockets of killing among loyalists of politicians themselves.

Nevertheless, the height of these problems came with the introduction of thuggery by politicians who wanted to win elections at all costs. This was a welcome but unfortunate development for the youth as many had no dependable means of livelihood because of the lack of jobs. This thuggery then developed into militia groups for the politicians. With time, the sponsors could neither cope with

---

[7] Ibid.

[8] Moses Tyosenda, "Economic Implication of insecurity in Sankara Area of Benue State." Unpublished symposium paper marking one year memorial of the death of Bishop Peter Adoboh, 2021, 1-2.

nor control these groups again. The militia groups then decided they could fend for themselves. The situation gave rise to robberies, kidnappings, killings of innocent citizens. Sometimes it was one militia group against another.[9]

Another reason for insecurity in the Sankara axis is the phenomenon of Fulani herders. The Tiv are farmers, while the Fulani are pastoralists. When Fulani graze on the fertile Sankara land, they destroy not only the farmlands but the crops. This has frequently resulted in skirmishes and eventual killings, and displacement of people. This development resulted in the enactment of the anti-open grazing law by the Benue State government. The Fulani's have resisted the law, and their reaction against it has been that of more attacks and killings displacement on farmers in Benue and Nassarawa state.

Boundary adjustment has also been a knotty issue. With the creation of Taraba state, some Tiv areas were taken to Taraba. Those indigenous people are now facing discrimination, sometimes being treated as settlers who must return to Benue State. This has often resulted in border crises.[10].

Just like the killing of Mohammed Yusuf aggravated Boko Haram in the Northeast, the gruesome murder of Terwase Akwaza (Gana) by the Nigerian Army on September 8, 2020, sparked a killing spree, by his supporters. He had been on his way from Katsina-Ala to Makurdi in a motorcade with traditional and religious leaders for amnesty. Prominent amongst those who were killed during this period are; Rev. Fr. Ferdinand Ngugban, a priest of Katsina-Ala diocese who was working at St. Paul's Parish Ayetwar; Dr. Terkula Suswam, the immediate elder brother to Sena-

---

9 Atser, *Op cit.*, 2.

10 Michael Mchia, "Insecurity in Katsina-Ala diocese." Unpublished symposium paper marking one year memorial of the death of Bishop Peter Adoboh, 2021, 3.

tor Gabriel Suswam; and other traditional rulers, Church leaders, civil servants, and so many other people within Sankara area. This has also given birth to another group that is fighting against the Gana group.[11]

From the above, one can easily see the development of the roots of criminality in the Sankara area. Moses Tyosenda has graphically captured it thus:

> The crime narrative in Sankara has changed. What used to be a band of militia with the acclaimed ideology of repelling external aggression in favour of their people gradually metamorphosed into a league of organised kidnappers, armed robbers, hired assassins, cross-border criminals, saboteurs as well as agents of subversion, espionage, and oppression.[12]

Adam Francis chronicled a list of some victims. In Zaki-Biam, the CEO of Light of Grace Hospital Dr Ndulue, and his pregnant wife were kidnapped, in the same manner as was Mr Emenike, Alhaji Mukaila, Mr Jude, and wife to the CEO of Rank oil.[13] Traditional rulers affected include Tyoor Awuha Alev, Zaki Ishom Shidi, Tyoor Aqua Alabar killed, and three of his five kindred heads: Zaki Orza Ahoo, Zaki Tyavzua Ayom, and Zaki Baja Anungwa. In the same vein, Zaki Kwaghhii and Zaki Shiinongo Agbatse were eliminated.[14]

Others also gruesomely murdered were Politicians, notable academics or their family members as well as doctors and clergymen, namely: Barrister Jande of the Law faculty, Benue State Uni-

---

11 Ibid.

12 Tyosenda, "Economic Implication of insecurity in Sankara Area of Benue State." 2.

13 Adam Francis *Orsankera hingir inyamtoho: Mkengese u hiihii.* (An unpublished poetry anthology, 2021), 4.

14 Ibid.

versity; Julius Ugah (Judas) of College of Education, Katsina-Ala; Elder Atodza Hindan, Elder Simon Chaverkper, Hon Mkperanga You, Hon Douglas Begha, ASP Linus Ugbor, Dr Udoo Angough, Hon Eric Asema, Mr Tavershima Achinge, Mr Terhemen Baso, and Chief Dr Terkula Suswam (the Zegeiwanger I Tiv).[15]

In cases where a ransom is demanded, figures are rarely reported. But ransoms running into millions of naira have allegedly been paid, thus, directly impoverishing families of the affected persons. Quite appalling and no less frightening, there have been incidents of reckless desecration of worship centers, robbing and molesting priests or ministers of God, and, to make things worse, the sacrilegious killing of Fr Ferdinand Ngugban.[16]

The Church's Peace, Dialogue and Mediation Strategy

On assumption of office as the chief shepherd of the diocese, Most Rev. Peter I. Adoboh encountered a diocese beset with series of abduction, kidnapping with demand for heavy ransom from abductors. The level of thievery had graduated from dark hours to broad daylight robbery within Katsina-Ala town and across the diocese. The climax of this was the abduction of Mr Aondowase Mnyim, a fuel dealer, in the presence of a divisional police officer (DPO) with his two policemen in Katsina-Ala town.[17] This threw the whole town into total fear and panic.

To facilitate peacebuilding and to return peace to Sankara, Bishop Adoboh embarked on a Peace initiative project. He engaged the youth, the political class, religious leaders, and traditional rulers through dialogue, consultations, negotiations, in an

15 Ibid.

16 Tyosenda, "Economic Implication of insecurity in Sankara Area of Benue State." 3.

17 Michael Mchia, "Insecurity in Katsina-Ala diocese." 14.

appeal for peace. He started consultation with Terwase Akwaza, popularly known as Gana, and his cohorts.[18] He convened a meeting with prominent sons and daughters of Sankara extraction at the Cathedral. Bishop Adoboh later moved into the hinterland to have personal contact with various militia leaders and their groups. He visited Gbishe (Gana's village) and was hosted in Gana's school.

Following was a visit to Zaki-Biam in Ukum under Igbur Kusugh, where the bishop talked with the group. Finally, he moved to Anyiin in Logo, where he met with Kumaiin, the militia group leader.[19]. After a series of personal visits and contacts with these groups, the bishop prevailed on the youth to surrender their weapons to embrace peace. Governor Gabriel Suswam was so helpful and supportive towards this peace initiative project that the youths agreed on a joint meeting scheduled at the residence of Governor Gabriel Suswam in Katsina-Ala in 2015. After the meeting at Katsina-Ala, the youths agreed to surrender their weapons. At this period, the government of Benue State, under the leadership of Governor Samuel Ortom, stepped in with the amnesty program.[20]

Bishop Adoboh had an undying passion for peaceful relations and was dedicatedly involved in peace building in Sankara land. The situation in Sankara could have been worse were it not for his timely, constant, and fatherly interventions. Unfortunately, Adoboh's episcopate from February 23, 2013, to February 14, 2020, was met with many challenges that hindered the implementation of primary evangelisation in the Catholic Diocese of Katsina-Ala. These challenges include insecurity, paucity of funds, insufficiency of priests, and the ill health which eventually took

---

18 Ibid. 5.

19 Ibid. 8.

20 Ibid.

his life.[21] Most Rev. William Avenya, the apostolic administrator of Katsina-Ala, has continued to engage the various arms of Sankara society, appealing for peace and seeking ways to resolve the conflicts. Besides various workshops for Traditional Rulers and the faithful of the Katsina-Ala diocese, the bishop organised the Bishop's Unity Tournament as an avenue for recreation and fraternity. He purchased town shuttle buses to facilitate movement Katsina-Ala town, among other peace initiatives.

Implications on the Development of Katsina-Ala Diocese

Socio-economic Implication

Insecurity within the Katsina-Ala diocese has aggravated the suffering of Sankara people and made the poor even more vulnerable. It has discouraged local and foreign investments, resulting in losing lives and property and has distorted economic values. For instance, in March 2021, there was an attack on Chinese expatriates (foreign investors) while working to establish a company at Gbaka-Wari in Kundav ward, Ukum Local Government Area. One Chinese engineer was shot dead on the spot, others wounded, and bundled away for ransom. This was aside from two security officers who suffered gruesome murder at the hands of the same criminals. The situation continues to dim any hope of employment for youth in the area even as commercial centers (market) are sometimes held hostage by the miscreants for significant periods without intervention from any security agency.[22]

---

21 Moses Igba, "Primary Evangelisation: An Appraisal of the Vision and Mission of late Bishop Peter I. Adoboh." (Unpublished symposium paper marking one year memorial of the death of Bishop Peter Adoboh, 2021), 14.

22 Thaddeus Kaor, "The Drama of insecurity and its consequences on Sankara." (Unpublished symposium paper marking one year memorial of the death of Bishop Peter Adoboh, 2021), 3.

Attacks by herdsmen have forced farmers to flee and cluster in urban centers like Zaki-Biam, Tor-Donga, Peva, Katsina-Ala, etc., with little or nothing to eat. At the same time, they ponder helplessly the loss of their crops to herders right in the heart of the farming season. This trend threatens the future of agricultural productivity and overall economic development of the Sankara area.

The Benue state government's ban on *Okada* riders (commercial motorcyclists) and use of the *Ducknyash* (A brand of Toyota vehicle) as commercial transport means in the three local governments that formed the Sankara area, namely: Katsina-Ala, Ukum, and Logo have gravely impacted the youth of the area negatively. Most of those engaged in these modes of transportation have turned to ride the tricycles *(Keke)* the others have been banned. *Okada* riders, vulcanizers, motor mechanics, drivers, electronic technicians, traders, and even apprentices abandoned these critical vocations for *Keke*'s venture in their quest for daily bread. The overall economic activity that hitherto existed and provided more economic inclusion of youths in the area has been regressed.[23].

Insecurity has also affected academics. We can recall a case when on a Monday, March 20, 2017, the late Antyo Anyam, a bandit or killer, popularly known as *Anyam U due* with a team of armed bandits invaded Zaki-Biam in search of his adversary, late Terungwa Igbawua, also known as Orlando of Tse Anjondo in Ukum LGA. The sporadic shooting of the armed team took the lives of many school students (pupils) who were returning from schools after closure. The team also destroyed many property, from the Yam Market area to areas around the roundabout close to the main market in Zaki-Biam.[24] Such killings of humans affected

---

23 Ibid. 4.

24 Felix Tsebee, Oral interview Zaki Biam, 2019.

schools, skills development, and health activities. These, in turn, affected human capital development and impaired productivity which is an economic indicator.

Pastoral Development

The Church is one social group that has greatly suffered from the negative impact of insecurity in Sankara. Many of the churches, particularly in the urban areas, became internally displaced camps, where people ran to. The burden of feeding them and providing other social amenities rested on the Parish houses, with their meager resources. This has hampered the growth of those parishes.

Insecurity has resulted in the closure of churches and parishes. The gruesome murder of Fr Ferdinand Ngugban at St Paul's Parish Ayetwar resulted in the shutdown of the parish by the diocese. In a similar development, crises at St John the Evangelist, Kasar forced the priests and parishioners to run away. The priests' residence was vandalised and pilfered, and the parish boy's quarters alongside other houses within the parish burnt down, thereby shutting down the parish. Other parishes like St Margaret Tor-donga, St John's Parish Gbishe, and Harga were all deserted. In fact, in the whole of Tor-donga deanery, only St Michael's parish Abaji functioned at a time with many internally displaced persons. Some outstation churches under St Gabriel's parish Agbanyi have also been closed down. This situation paralysed pastoral activities and affected the development of Katsina-Ala diocese.

The scenario has affected the pastoral and financial activities of the diocese ranging from reduced church offerings to inadequate maintenance of the agents of evangelisation and preventing developmental projects in the diocese. Those who have little to sell cannot find people to buy at reasonable prices. This has negatively affected the pastoral drive of the diocese. Even those with the relative means are afraid to come out openly to support the Church for fear of being attacked. This has thwarted charity and has instilled fear in the people. Some affluent lay members of the diocese have even fled from the diocese to other places for safety.

Way Forward

As the harbinger of peace, the Church in Katsina-Ala must intensify prayers and re-strategise her evangelisation strategies to target youth and political elites. Conscious propagation of the Christian values, like the inviolable dignity and respect for human life and property, should be projected. Workshops and youth programs to teach youths about the value of peace and the dangers of violence must be sustained. Gospel values and family life, as well as responsible parenthood, must be revived. As part of the Catholic Church in Tivland, our current situation in the Sankara axis calls for the following:

Job Creation and Youth Empowerment: Key to Peaceful Sustainability

It is common knowledge that there has been Political exploitation and disempowerment of the youth in Tiv land and the Sankara area. Tiv political history has shown that Tiv sons and daughters have always been used as political thugs to engender violence in politics and then abandoned by the political elites without empowerment in entrepreneurship, education, agriculture, and politics. No wonder youth look at guns and weapons as a form of empowerment and employ them to kill and engage in criminality.[25] The political class's attitude has made youth erroneously believe that armed

[25] Godwin Bagu, "Beating Swords into Ploughshares in Tivland Isaiah 2:4," (Unpublished paper, Prayer Pilgrimage for Peace in Tiv Land, 2020), 14.

robbery, political thuggery, or violence is more profitable than farming and education.

There must be a conscious effort to beating swords into ploughshares. This requires a new attitude where monies hitherto used to buy guns are henceforth used for scholarships. Also, such monies must be uses to build cottage industries for meaningful employment of the youth. Notably, such monies should provide soft loans for youth to begin small-scale businesses, where agro seeds and grains are given to engage in productive farming. Militia-armed youth should be given valid amnesty and rehabilitated for the common good. It requires a new mentality where youth will grow from being boys of a political godfather to responsible men who are helpful to themselves and their families. There must be a paradigm shift from seeing our youth as ready tools for exploitation to ready tools for empowerment, from treating them as objects for use and disposal to human beings worth investing in and harnessing their prosperous energies for productive ventures to enhance nation-building and community development.[26]

Dialogue and Reasonable Negotiation Rather than Violence

Restoring peace and security in Sankara requires a new attitude, where might is not seen as right. The fiercest of wars are won on the dialogue table and not on the battlefield. Pope John Paul II has cautioned that:

> Human affairs must be dealt with humanely, not with violence. Tensions, rivalries, and conflicts must be settled by reasonable negotiations and not by force. Opposing ideologies must confront each other in a climate of dialogue and free discussion. He cautions further that the legitimate interests of particular groups

[26] Ibid., 19.

> must also consider the legitimate interests of the other groups involved and the demands of the higher common good. Recourse to arms cannot be considered a suitable means for settling conflicts.[27]

The same idea is captured by Pope John XXIII thus: any disputes which may arise between nations must be resolved by negotiation and agreement, and not by recourse to arms."[28] This is imperative because, as observed by Pope Pius XII: "Nothing is lost by peace; everything may be lost by war."[29]

Enforcement of Just Punishment and Restitution

The true path to peace requires a just punishment for an offense committed in order to deter others and enhance peace. Where a just punishment is not served to offenders, the likelihood of recurrence is inevitable. Restitution seeks to correct vice and seeks after justice. Justice is giving to each what is due to them. Justice is a virtue by which we respect the rights of others and seek to promote harmony between persons based upon the common good. This must be pursued in Sankara for peace to reign.

Peace Must be Built on Truth

For peace to return to Sankara territory, we must embrace respect for truth and offer forgiveness to receive peace. As Pope John Paul II taught, forgiveness is a free act of love in its truest and highest form. However, precisely because it is an act of love, it has

---

27 Pope John Paul II *Message for the celebration of the Day of Peace*, January 1, 1979, #1.

28 Pope John XXIII, *Pacem en Terris* #126.

29 Pius XII's broadcast message August 24, 1939, *Acta Apostolicae Sedis* 31

its intrinsic demands; the first of which is respect for the truth.[30] Where lies and falsehood are sown, suspicion and division flourish. Forgiveness, far from precluding the search for truth, actually requires it.

The evil which has been done must be acknowledged and as far as possible corrected. It is precisely this requirement that has led to the establishment in various parts of the world of appropriate procedures for ascertaining the truth regarding crimes between ethnic groups or nations as the first step towards reconciliation. The Benue state government had granted amnesty to repentant armed youth, but can we say the amnesty was built on truth by both the government and those granted amnesty? The nexus between truth and reconciliation explains why truth and reconciliation commissions are established to heal wounds in advanced climes.

The Role of the Government

The government should emulate the Church in Sankara by engaging in targeted youth activities such as the Unity Cup, introduced by the late Bishop Adoboh and sustained by Bishop Avenya, to bring lasting peace to the area. Again, the government should live up to its responsibility by paying workers and avoid harsh economic and exploitative policies that bring excessive hardship to the land. The proliferation of arms should be checked by the government and security agencies.

---

30 Pope John Paul II, "Offer forgiveness and receive peace," Message for the celebration of the XXX world day of peace 1997, #5.

Chapter Nine

The Catholic Laity in Tivland

Francis K. Ode[1]

Introduction

As a term, "laity" derives from the Greek *laikos*, which means "of the people." *Laikos* is a derivative of *laos* meaning "the people" at large. Thus, the word laity simply describes all of the faithful who have not received Holy Orders including the professed religious. Lakeland defines a layperson as "a baptised Christian, gifted by the Spirit with a responsibility for the mission of the Church that will be carried out through the particular human qualities and gifts that this individual possesses.[2] At the close of his earthly ministry, Jesus commissioned his apostles to "Go then to all peoples everywhere, and make them disciples: baptise them in the name of the Father and the Son and the Holy Spirit, and teach them to obey everything I have commanded you" (Mt 28:19-20).

1 Sir Francis K. Ode, is a Knight of the Catholic Church and of one of the foremost families to embrace the Catholic faith in Tivland. His father, Bonaventure Kange Ode, was a pioneer Catechist at St. Joseph Korinya from 1935- 1952. His brother, late Fr Robert Ode also served as Parish Priest in Korinya from 1978-1982.

2 Paul Lakeland, *Catholicism at Crossroads: How the Laity Can Save the Church* (New York: Continuum, 2007), 34.

Canon law defines members of Christ's faithful as:

> ...those who, since they are incorporated in Christ through baptism, are constituted the people of God. For this reason, they participate in their way in the priestly, prophetic, and kingly office of Christ. According to their particular condition, they are called each to exercise the mission God entrusted to the Church to fulfill in the world (Can. 204:1).[3]

In her wisdom and quest for clarity, the Church classified Christ's faithful into clerics and laypeople. These are also called clergy and laity, and their grouping is based on the nature of their call in the salvific mission. Canon law expresses that:

> By divine institution, amongst Christ's faithful, there are in the church sacred ministers, who in law are called clerics, the others are called laypeople.[4]

Whereas the clerics are ordained sacred ministers of the Church, the laypeople include the religious and non-ordained people who carry out the Church's affairs in the secular sphere.

Arrival of the Catholic Faith in Tivland

Documented history indicates several attempts to bring the Catholic faith into Tivland, with multiple entry points. In the southern part of Tivland, the first significant success was recorded in 1924 with the arrival of the first expatriate missionary priest, Rev. Fr Vincent Douvry.[5] On arrival in Makurdi, he established a

---

3 Canon 204:1.

4 Canon 207:1.

5 Cf. Fr Kuhwa Indyer, Cssp. "The Contribution of Holy Ghost Fathers and Brothers to the Birth and Growth of Makurdi Diocese" in Shagbaor F. Wegh (Ed) (2010) *Catholic*

small temporary station where he engaged a catechist of Ibo extraction to carry out preliminary missionary assignments. By the middle of 1930, the temporary station assumed a permanent status with four missionaries; two priests and two brothers.

This team commenced their missionary work in earnest with the building of a Church, saying daily masses, engaging youth for education at the established missionary school, the teaching of catechism and other religious instruction which led to baptism; as well as the teaching of professional trades to members of the immediate community. Gradually, a Catholic Christian community was developing to become the propelling point for evangelisation throughout Tivland and beyond.

The arrival of the Roman Catholic Church undoubtedly stirred up conflicts with other denominations already settled in Tivland. In particular, the Dutch Reformed Church Mission (DRCM) engaged in a campaign of calumny against the Catholic Church when it became evident that more people were drifting to activities of the Catholic Church, leading to their neglect of the Reformed Mission. The Catholic missionaries withstood these challenges and made inroads into the entire Benue Province with the arrival of more priests, baptizing, and opening new churches and worshiping centers.

However, the early missionary work was amputated by the outbreak of the Second World War in 1939, caused by the world's socio-political disorder. This demanded the withdrawal of Germans from all English-occupied territories, Nigeria inclusive. By the end of the war in 1945, the vacuum created by the exit of the Germans was gradually filled up with the posting of Monsignor James Hagan CSSP as the first Prefect Apostolic along with three priests to take charge of the work in Benue. These were all of the Holy

---

Diocese of Makurdi at 50: A Celebration of Service to Humanity (Makurdi: Seffers Academic Press Ltd).

Ghost Order. The principal undertaking by the second missionary team was in the area of opening more churches and establishing primary schools in the hinterland, and teaching catechism and other religious instructions that resulted in the conversion of more people to Christianity.

As the task was gradually extended into the hinterland, there was the need for a revised administrative structure that would accommodate the additional pastoral needs. First-generation parishes were created at Naka (1931), Korinya (1934), Gboko (1938), etc., with expansive outstations for each.[6] As priests were assigned to these parishes, the Church went closer to the people. It became necessary to involve the laypeople who would support the priests for the ensuing additional pastoral work. These were engaged in different fields but prominently as catechists and teachers who, though not well educated, were working under the strict supervision of the priests in their various pastoral engagements.

The gradual progress achieved by the Church in the whole of the Benue area gave rise to her promotion to the status of a diocese on April 2, 1959, with initial headquarters in Otukpo. However, the headquarters was renamed and moved to Makurdi on June 28, 1960, with her chief shepherd as Bishop James Hagan CSSP. On his resignation in 1968, Most Rev. D. J. Murray, CSSP, was appointed as his replacement. Bishop Murray's tenure experienced developments in pastoral programs that enthused more laypeople about Christianity and further drew their participation in the Catholic faith. The Church in the then Makurdi Diocese, which covered all of Tivland and beyond, recorded a spiritual boom arising from an increased number of priests and religious, admission of more indigenous students into the major and junior seminaries,

6 Ibid.18-20.

the establishment of educational and medical health institutions, establishment of religious institutions, increase in the population of Catholic Christians, greater involvement by the lay faithful in the mission of the Church, and reorganisation of pious societies and sodalities under the Laity Council as their apex body.

This boom enabled the creation of a deanery structure for a more effective administration of the diocese. As the scope of evangelising work became heavier, more responsibilities were devolved. Ill-health would however, not allow Bishop Murray to continue the increasing arduous task of pastoral work, and in 1988 an indigenous priest, Rev. Fr Athanasius Atule Usuh was appointed as a Coadjutor Bishop to assist him. It became apparent that the dream for a Tiv Church was gradually being realised. Most Rev. Bishop D. J. Murray resigned on June 2, 1989, handed over his duties to Bishop Athanasius Usuh, who eventually was officially installed as the first indigenous Bishop of Makurdi Diocese and third in succession on October 21, 1989.

The Catholic Laity in Tivland

The mobilisation of the lay faithful towards active participation as members of the body of Christ in Tivland is indeed coterminous with the missionaries' arrival. On arrival, the missionaries needed the help and support of some faithful local assistants as interpreters, catechists, mission support staff, and certain families who would serve as their base for subsequent activity. In relating the history of the early missionaries in the Korinya area of Tivland, Azer Beke notes,

> The Holy Ghost Fathers were assisted by catechists and cooks who always accompanied them in their work of preaching the gospel in the rural areas. And to reach the rural areas, tours were often undertaken by these Revd Fathers who traveled on bicycles

or foot through narrow footpaths and at times crossed streams on the back of the catechist or the cook.[7]

Notable among the cooks in Korinya was Mr. Joseph Ajayi Ade, while James Azuana Dabo was the pioneer catechist, followed by Bonaventure Kange Ode, Patrick Yanyam Iber, and Michael Shiko. In Udei, it took the sacrifices of Michael Kinga Upaa for the missionaries to set up the mission there. Each location in Tivland had such notable and invaluable collators who should not be forgotten for their roles in the early life of the Tiv Church.

As parishes sprang up in Tivland, the lay faithful organised their support for evangelisation collectively as individuals or pious mushroom groups. Bishop Donal Murray CSSp, who for a time was the sole Catholic Bishop responsible for all of Tivland, envisaged more responsibility for the Church in Tivland, resulting from a gradual rise in the Catholic Christian population with the attendant growth in needs for pastoral care. It became indispensable for the bishop to engage the laity in a more coordinated manner for a more aggressive evangelisation.

Drawing from the Second Vatican Council which had just concluded, especially its decree on the role of the laity in evangelisation mission, he identified two eminent Catholics who had shown proficiency in mobilisation and leadership, namely Mr. Alfred Amodu KSM, then Commissioner for Education in Benue State, and Mr D. D. Dodo then Principal of Mount Saint Michaels Aliade to take up the responsibility of mobilising the laity into an effective and active body. These two further identified and conscripted a few people to work with them and were inaugurated as the maiden Diocesan Council at a concelebrated Mass by the Bishop and all the Priests in August 1976.

---

7 Azer Beke, A Citation of St Joseph's Parish Korinya, September 7, 2014, 7.

Following the inauguration, the laity commenced their task with tours and awareness visits to all the parishes and soliciting cooperation and support for the work of the Church in the diocese. By the close of their three-year tenure, many tours had been undertaken to parishes; the priests were according gradual support; more Pious Societies and sodalities sprang up; increased membership of the organised groups was recorded; participation at both parish and diocesan events became impressive, and attendance of national meetings was stepped up; fundraising activities for pastoral work became more regular in churches and gave better results.

After four successive administrations of the Diocesan Executive Council, some skirmishes persisted, indicating that the Council had lost its direction. The then Bishop, Most Rev. Athanasius Usuh, in August 2003, suspended the Council for three years, after which a caretaker committee was appointed and inaugurated in the year 2006. The committee headed by Mrs Lucy Z. Aluor MFR was given the mandate to reorganise the Laity Council at all levels in the Diocese and restore its image in line with the expectations of the Church in Makurdi Diocese, requiring all societies and sodalities to reflect the valid message of Christ in the conduct of their affairs.

The strategies adopted in the reorganisation process were: holding consultations with the clergy, holding quarterly meetings, annual seminars, and workshops; formation and nurturing of societies and organisations, reorganising and supervising elections at the deaneries and parishes: There was also more active participation at Provincial and National Laity Council meetings. During the tenure of the caretaker committee, the idea of the Laity Council being the apex body of all the pious societies and sodalities was also pursued and gradually accepted.

These measures took a while to elicit positive results. However, by 2012, better cooperation was established between the clergy, lay faithful, and council members themselves at all levels. Having been dissolved after six years of intensive work, the caretaker committee had its tenure extended for another three years in a substantive capacity, and a new EXCO was elected to consolidate on the gains that were made. Bishop Usuh, while acknowledging these gains had this to say:

> In the last twenty-five years, most development projects executed have been financed through the generosity of our active laity both as individuals and as groups… The people's generous disposition is further demonstrated in the enormous gifts I receive every year during Christmas. It is still with the laity that the Church in Makurdi has what is necessary for divine worship, social work, and sustenance of her Pastoral agents.[8]

At the expiration of the three years, two executive councils were elected consecutively under Noble Damian Kpemgwa KSJI, JP, and Mr Daniel Kwaza, JP, respectively. These two also ensured a steady growth of laity in the then Diocese of Makurdi.

With the creation of the dioceses of Gboko and Katsina-Ala in 2012, sustained participation by members of pious societies and sodalities has been tremendous. It accounts for the achievements recorded by the Catholic Church in Tivland today under the broad umbrella of the laity. The Diocesan Laity Council in Makurdi Diocese is today led by Mr Daniel Kwaghza, while Mr. Francis Moji is the Chair for Gboko Diocese and Mr. Linus Vandefan for Katsina-Ala Diocese.

Some of the Pious societies and sodalities which are found in all dioceses in Tivland include; Catholic Women Organisation, Catholic Men's Organisation, Catholic Youth Organisation, Order of Knights (St Mulunba, St John's, Papal Knights, and St Columbus), Sacred Heart of Jesus and Immaculate Heart of Mary, Legion

---

8 Bishop A.A. Usuh, *A Call to Service and Renewal: Post-Synodal Exhortation*. (Makurdi, 2012), 81.

of Mary, Catholic Biblical Movement, Association of Lay Readers, Choir, Purgatorian Society, St Rita of Cascia, Ministers of Hospitality, Holy Infant Jesus, Block Rosary Crusade, Confraternity of Most Holy Rosary, Holy family, Association of Catholic Nurses, Association of Catholic Youth Corpers, Precious Blood, Catholic Charismatic Renewal, St Vincent de Paul, etc. All these are coordinated at the respective Dioceses by the Diocesan Laity Councils, and in them, there exist various professionals and technicians that offer various services to the Church's work of evangelisation.

Hopes for the Future

Although the evangelisation strides by the Catholic Church in the past hundred years have made a positive impact in Tivland, the role of the laity is, most often, limited to their contribution in the form of *3T's* (Time, Talent and Treasure), in the life of the Church. However, looking at the evolving events in the society that constitute trials and threats to the proclamation of the message of Jesus Christ, it will be necessary for the Catholic Church in Tivland to consider novel ways of engaging the laity, which are enshrined in the documents of the Second Vatican Council.

Firstly, it is crucial to articulate the need for co-responsibility in ministry and evangelisation between Christ's faithful and the clergy in Tivland. As reflected in the local languages, the Catholic Church is seen as that of the priests in most of Africa. Among the Tiv, for example, the Roman Catholic Church is referred to as "adua u fada" (Father's Church), and the hierarchy in some cases functions as if the Church were indeed theirs and the laity merely tenants in the "father's house." Patriarchy in society intensifies the lay faithful's experience of exclusion and deference in the Church, since Church authority, and by extension decision making, is associated with the sacrament of Orders which is limited to the ordained in the Catholic Church.[9]

Indeed, for example, the Second Vatican Council maintains that since the laity share in the Church's mission, all Christ's faithful have the right to promote and support apostolic action, by their initiative, undertaken according to their state and condition. Indeed, Paragraph 3 of Canon 212 of the Code of Canon Law asserts expressly that the laity "have the right, indeed at times the duty, in keeping with their knowledge, competence, and position, to manifest to the sacred pastors their views on matters which concern the good of the Church."[10] Being knowledgeable about their role will positively impact the faith value the laity will bring on their public witness in society, including active participation in politics and civil society for the common good.

Secondly, proper catechesis is urgently needed in the rising threat of Pentecostalism, which is fast-growing in Tivland and worldwide. The youth who are the seed for the future of the Catholic Church are the primary targets, and the glaring reality of losing a significant number of Catholic Christians to other faiths is today too common. A deliberate strategy of adopting new methods of pastoral outreach, attending to the needs of the teeming youth in an environment of poverty, want, and exclusion is non-negotiable for the Catholic Church at this point.

Thirdly, since the activities of the Catholic Church are fast-growing and embracing more people in the rural communities

---

9 Gabriel T. Wankar, "The Laity and Decision-Making" in *Practical Ways of Engaging the Laity in Nigeria*. Daniel Asue Ed. (Iperu-Remo: Ambassador Publications, 2016) 31.

10 *Lumen Gentium no. 31,* as quoted by Wankar, "The Laity and Decision-making," 36.

of Tivland, the present methods of communicating the Christian message should be re-evaluated along the lines of the benefits of digitalization. It is no secret now that people show particular interest in electronic presentations. In almost all the localities in Tivland, one would find one person with a television set and decoders powered by small power plants. Some are in established viewing centers that operate various programs, especially soccer which has become a source to earn a living for enterprising young people. Suppose the communication directorates of the Catholic dioceses in Tivland take advantage of these. Though the current efforts are commendable, the present societal changes suggest that the Church must also match gallantly in all directions to engage well.

Fourthly, given the level of poverty and the underdevelopment in Tiv land, it is most desirable for the Tiv Church to evolve efficient diocesan financial policies to assuage the current financial burden on the laity in the form of levies and collections. It is a fact that most Tiv Catholics prioritise Church collections and levies over medical expenses, their feeding, and other personal comforts in an environment of want and squalor. Thus, while service to the Church should be a joyful privilege, it has gotten to a stage where it becomes a burden, and the laity only smiles in pretense at the numerous levies. It is imperative, therefore, for the Catholic Dioceses in Tivland to intensify efforts towards economic and financial self-reliance, through efficient investments of economic nature, whose returns will be used in service of the evangelising mission of the Church, instead of numerous levies and collections that sometimes keep members away from Church or become a burden.

Lastly, mechanisms for conflict resolution must be strengthened in the Tiv Catholic Church. Our bishops and clergy will lead by example of harmonious coexistence to earn the trust and respect to serve as referral points in times of discord among Christ's faithful. Since evangelisation involves different cadres of the society, the manifestation of occasional conflicts cannot be overruled. These could be influenced by cultural, economic, and political factors,

knowledge gaps, deficiency in upbringing, ill-health problems, etc., which can negatively impact relationships amongst the people of God. Once this is noticed in the system, it is necessary to resolve issues and ensure smoothness in evangelisation. A harmonious relationship, if neglected, may frustrate the work of evangelisation.

Conclusion

Evangelisation in Tivland has assumed a remarkable level due to the untiring efforts and sacrifices of the pioneering missionaries. Their efforts and those of the indigenous Christ's faithful contributed to the success of evangelisation in Tivland, which gave birth to additional four (4) dioceses in the territory that the Makurdi Diocese initially covered. The tiny seed of evangelisation sown about 100 years ago, has grown over the years in Tivland and the territories contiguous to it, in such a manner that it can be likened to the biblical parable of Jesus to his followers about the mustard seed; which though the smallest of seeds, when sown by a man in his field, grows up into the biggest of plants, and becomes a tree that provides in its branches a resting place for the birds.

The positive outcomes of this vibrant evangelic mission in Tivland are shared worldwide with the universal Church, which affirms the parable of Jesus about the mustard seed. With all joy and pride, it can be said that the way and stage Christianity was in Tivland to where it is now in 100 years is an excellent achievement by the Catholic Church in Tivland and, by extension, Nigeria. Creating additional Dioceses out of one diocese in a hundred years is a significant milestone in the history of Christianity in Nigeria and calls for special thanks to God's mercies. It reflects the people's embrace of the Catholic faith and is a testimony of the hard work of the early missionaries and their lay collaborators. Our prayer is that the collective roles played by Christ's faithful in the evangelising mission in Tivland will continue to bear fruits and redirect humanity to the way of eternal salvation.

Chapter Ten

The Catholic Women Organisation and Its Impact in Tivland

Member George-Genyi & Mariam Ejikeme[1]

Introduction

This chapter takes a historical survey of the Catholic Women Organisation's (CWO) establishment and its activities in the Church in Tivland in the last one hundred years. It is trite knowledge that the history of the existence of the Catholic Church in Tivland cannot be complete without stating the enormous contributions of the catholic women in terms of their talents, time, and treasure to every endeavour of the Church.

It is also interesting to note that Jesus had a heart for women, as the Bible clarifies, Women were the first to be at the foot of the cross and the last to leave (Lk 24).[2] They moved with Jesus during his ministry and supported him with all they had (Mt 26:6-14). They were also the first that Jesus sent to inform the men about

---

1 Professor Member George-Genyi, a devout Catholic and active member of the CWO, is of the Benue State University Makurdi. Mariam Ejikeme attended Nativity Private School Makurdi, and she holds a Bachelor of Arts Degree in History and Political Science for Ahmadu Bello University Zaria, a Master of Arts in History and Strategic Studies from the University of Lagos.

2 Damian Anyam, *Religion, Feminism, Gender Issues and National Development*. (Ibadan: Bright Integrated Publishers Limited, 2016).

His resurrection (Mt 28:9-10). Women indeed have been valid witnesses for the truth about Jesus. This is the scenario that we are bound to appreciate about the CWO in the Church in Tivland for over a century. Against this background, we also present the emergence of the Christian Church as a community of believers in the Lord Jesus Christ and his teachings. We can also identify these believers in several actions that are characteristics of their chosen state in life.

They are communal in disposition, breaking of one bread, baptism, charity, and support to the Church.[3] Mato talks about the mandate they had received to continue the work of Christ among men when he left physically on earth. He notes that it is keeping with Jesus' injunction and command to go and teach all nations that the missionaries traversed the length and breadth of the earth to bring the Good news to the people. This is the basis for the missionary activities that led to their coming to Tivland.

Generally, even in Nigeria, it was not until 1880 that the Catholic missionaries arrived in Nigeria from Calabar and Badagry and penetrated the different towns of Nigeria. Getting inland was initially a herculean task as the missionaries were confronted with tropical diseases such as malaria, yellow fever, and others. They also had to reckon with the language barrier, the dearth of infrastructure, the inhabitants' general hostilities towards strangers, and a new way of life.

This is the setting that characterized the attempt to bring Christianity, the good news to Tivland. Despite these challenges, the first Catholic Priests arrived in Makurdi in 1924 via the railway line that reached Makurdi from the Southern part of Nigeria. The

3 Clement Mato, "The Catholic Church in Tivland" in *Catholic Diocese of Makurdi at 50: A Celebration of Service to Humanity*. Shagbaor F. Wegh, Ed. (Makurdi: Sellers Academic Press Ltd, 2010).

Irish Holy Ghost Fathers had opened a mission in Ogoja in 1921 and had intended to use that as a springboard to establish their presence and evangelising mission in Makurdi. Fr Douvry was the first to undertake this assignment but was withdrawn by ill-health and was succeeded by Father Eugene Goetz. As the years progressed, many other missionaries arrived in Makurdi, and they had to work hard to cover grounds as late-comers to Tivland because other missionary groups were already on the ground, like the Dutch Reformed Church Mission (DRCM) who already were established at a village called Saai as early as 1911.

The Catholic Church in Tivland has indeed grown in leaps and bounds with great successes and challenges. In its development, several dioceses have been carved out of the original Makurdi diocese that was the seat of missionary activities. From then to now, the Church has grown both in membership and in the fields and areas requiring the divine touch of God, notably, education, health, justice, peace, and development, etc. The lay apostolates, societies, organisations, and sodalities have increased and have been veritable avenues for evangelisation and the expression of the catholic social teachings. The Catholic Women Organisation (CWO) has been one of the societies, and we will x-ray her contributions to the Church in the subsequent section.

With Bishop A.A. Usuh, the first indigenous Bishop who was installed on the 21st of October 1989, the Diocese stretched to the Camerouns, to Abuja, Igala land, and out of this vast space, he was able to get Rome to carve out Otukpo, Lafia, Katsina-Ala, Gboko dioceses and what is remaining of Makurdi diocese today.

The Catholic Women Organisation in Perspective

In his message to the World Union of Catholic Women Organisation (WUCWO) representatives, on the 27th of March 2020 on Mothers Day Celebration, Pope Francis rightly acknowledged that "it is the women who carry the church forward without holding any positions." Though the Catholic Church has it that women should be kept away from the pulpit, their commitments and contributions have remained highly noticeable by the Church. Historically, even in the secular world, women's associations have existed in the colonial era and were plausible platforms for economic, social, and political expressions for women and their causes. They were a strong voice against colonial imperialism and have continued to contribute towards nation-building. In 1943, Mrs Funmilayo Ransome Kuti, for example, established and headed the Abeokuta Women Union, a strong voice against obnoxious colonial policies. From the independence era in 1960, more Women Associations have sprung up and continued to act as mobilisers of other women to achieve desired objectives.

The idea of uniting leagues of Catholic Women throughout the world was conceived in 1910 by Madame de Velard. The various leagues of catholic women officially adopted the name World Union of Catholic Women Organisation in 1952, and from then, spread to many countries of Africa and other continents. In Nigeria, all the Catholic Dioceses have an organisation. As the name implies, the CWO is a faith-based gender bias organisation operating within the Catholic Church and has membership open to all catholic women from the age of eighteen and above who have embraced the sacramental life of the Church. It is one of the most prominent organisations in the Church, operating alongside the Catholic Men Organisation (CMO) and the Catholic Youth Organisation of Nigeria (CYON), and others. The Ecclesiastical hierarchy recognises that the CWO and its operations are in line with the acceptable guidelines of the Church. They are independent of partisan politics.

In Nigeria, the organisational structure begins with the National Council of Catholic Women Organisation (NCCWO), Nigeria, and this body is answerable to the Catholic Bishops Conference of Nigeria (CBCN). Provincial bodies are answerable to the respective provincial Archbishops with the assistance of all the Bishops in those provinces.[4] The Diocesan bodies follow the provincial and are answerable to the Bishops. The deaneries follow suit and are answerable to the Deans. The parish levels follow from there and are superintended by the parish priests. There are the zonal levels that are the closest to the women. All these inevitably owe allegiance to the WUCWO.[5]

The CWO in Tivland

The CWO in Tivland and its activities could form what Feese refers to as Catholic Women confraternities in the parishes under the auspices of the then Bishop, Most Rev. Donal J. Murray (CSSP). This Confraternity of Catholic Women (CCW) was engaged in apostolic work, evangelism, and charity. On the 14th of July 1975, the inaugural meeting of the CWO was held under the leadership of Mrs Susanna Ihur. Between 1979 and 1980, an elected Executive Council under the leadership of Lady Maria Feese (LSM) was formed with Rev. Fr Simon Ivever as the First Spiritual Adviser.[6] Their main objective then was the creation of awareness at the grassroots about the faith and the drive for membership recruitment.

These are indeed the main objectives of the CWO, namely to evangelise through outreach programs, empowerment of women, charity work to indigent members of the Church, uniting

---

4 F. Nzekwu, "Catholic Women: Sowers of Hope for the Common Good" in *Mystical Role Magazine*. Vol. 3. Issue 1. 2015.

5 Maria Feese, "The Catholic Women Organisation and its Work in Makurdi Diocese" in *Catholic Diocese of Makurdi at 50: A Celebration of Service to Humanity*. Shagbaor F. Wegh, Ed. (Makurdi: Selfers Academic Press Ltd., 2010).

6 Ibid.

all women and directing them for love, unity and peace, and to be a platform which women operate and participate fully in the affairs of the Church.

Since 1980, when Mama Maria Feese (LSM) was elected the first president of the DCWO in Makurdi, a succession chart with Lady Stella Grace Ogbaje, Hon. Lady Margaret Iyorember (LSM), Mrs Victoria Asom, Mrs Dorothy Atser-Igyuve, Lady Grace Adedzwa (LSM, JP), Lady Tessy Atser-Iwail, (KSJI, IY, AP, JP), and Lady Christiana Mayange, (LSM, AP, JP). With the creation of two more dioceses in Tivland, leadership has also emerged performing those responsibilities of the CWO at all levels of the dioceses. Since the creation of Gboko, Lady Victoria Gyado, Lady Felicia Congo, and Eunice Gungur have served as Diocesan Presidents to date, while Lady Dinnah Ankaau, Mrs Roseline Aye, and Roseline Dooga for Katsina-Ala diocese.

What Has Been the Impact of the CWO?

An assessment of the impact of the CWO in Tivland must be done within the context of its objectives of the operation.

In an interview with a former Diocesan President of the CWO on the 22nd of September, 2021, Lady Tessy Atser-Iwail outlined the major success story of the CWO in Tivland to be that of evangelisation within the context of the guided hand of the Church. The organisation's leadership at the different levels has engaged in creative ways of wooing participation by members and encouraging lukewarm members to return to active participation. Meetings are held regularly and to ensure inclusiveness, and visits are made to sick and distressed members.

The CWO has taken the gospel message to the prisons, orphanages, and the poor and offered prayers and succour to the marginalised. Secondly, the CWO has continued to promote the spiritual growth and development of their members and family generally.[7] In the Catholic Dioceses in Tivland, the CWO's slogan has remained, CWO, (*ka mtuunuum make church man make ya*), meaning CWO, pillars of the Church and the family. This has been exemplified by the leadership at all levels undertaking spiritual development activities such as retreats, Bible verses recitation, end of year vigils, publication of magazines, corporal works and spiritual works of mercy, participation at cathedraticum, Chrism Mass, WUCWO annual recollection, the inclusion of the prayer of Francis of Assisi for peace in Benue State usually sang at every CWO meeting. Participation in calls by the Benue State Government to pray for peace and progress of our land.

Thirdly, the CWO has continued to contribute financially and materially to the growth of the Church and Tivland. Through their levies and contributions, the CWO has always contributed enormously to the causes of the Church. The Church's hierarchy has always acknowledged this fact and clearly stated that the saving ministry would have been constrained but for the support that they receive from the women. The CWO has, over the years, given financial support and gifts to Bishops, seminaries, health institutions.

They have contributed mass vestments, vehicles, and many other items to the Church at different points in the history of the Church. They have offered their talents at Committees and made seminal presentations and interventions at different fora in the Church and the Church. They have contributed to priests and their parents (the three Dioceses have an association with the priests/sisters parents, and it is a brainchild of the CWO). During Easter and Christmas seasons, the CWO usually extends her jar of oil to

[7] R Ahura, R. "Catholic Women: Carriers of Living Water to a World that Thirsts for Peace" in *Mirror of Justice Magazine.* Issue 3 Vo. 1. 2018.

priests, indigent members, and the disadvantaged in society. The CWO is indeed a strong pillar for the Church and the family.

In addition, the organisation is also involved in offering support to their members who aspire to political office; they celebrate their members who have achieved success by way of appointments. They have established various developmental and social services outfits such as schools, St Claire schools in Makurdi diocese, CWO Business plaza, and Hostels in Gboko Diocese, acquiring land for development in Kastina-Ala diocese. The CWO in the 3 Dioceses has acquired buses for easy evangelisation work. They have acquired land for development, and they usually mobilise members for political awareness and participation. In collaboration with others in the Church, the organisation has continued to organise and teach the youth and others on good morals, church doctrines, marriage, and family life.

Conclusion and Recommendations

As the WUCWO anthem indicates, women generally and the CWO in Tivland is "working to build a better world where the dove of peace can rest on every side." As we reminisce on the last one hundred years of Catholicism in Tivland, we are confronted with a history inundated with the active participation of women in the Catholic Church under the auspices of the Catholic Women Organisation. This body has continued to colate with the salvific mission of the Church as always promoted by its Teaching Authority. This women's umbrella body has continued to mobilize, create awareness, educate and promote women's participation in the affairs of the Church and, by extension, the Tiv nation. The membership has remained a veritable source of spiritual growth of the women, children, and promotion of family values and funding source for the numerous activities and projects of the Church, especially in its social teaching.

We note with concern that over the world, women constitute a considerable percentage of the world population referred to as the poor and vulnerable, those who live in conditions that are dehumanizing, degrading, and unacceptable. They are poor and marginalised and earn low incomes. This is the lot of the majority of Tiv women who have overwhelming membership in the Catholic Church. Interestingly, these women under the platform of the CWO have contributed more than 70% of the resource base and support to the Church despite their financial and material disadvantage. This has enabled the Church to embark on capital projects in health, education, infrastructure, etc. Therefore, it is recommended that the Church's hierarchy need to devise creative ways by which these women will benefit from these developmental initiatives and reduce the burdens they carry from the levies and taxes they pay to the Church.

We further propose that the Church makes conscious efforts to train the women in skills acquisition, leadership, and self-reliance ventures. This will uplift the women and place them on a pedestal of self-development, and they will become more valuable to themselves, their families, the Church, and society

In a world where the United Nations, through the 2015 Sustainable Development Goals (SDGs), specifically Goal 15, seeks to achieve gender Equality and empowerment of women and girls by 2030 by all nations through programs and advocacy places emphasis on sustainable development in the context of poverty education, self-reliance, gender equity, and equality, the Catholic Church in Tivland in the 21st century cannot be left out as the world is headed in the direction of ensuring meaningful existence for the men and women. This is the task also for the hierarchy of the Catholic Church in Tivland!

What is remaining is for the continued partnership and cordiality that should be sustained in the years ahead for the growth and development of the Church and Tiv society in general.

Chapter Eleven

The Catholic Church and Youth Development In Tivland

Richard Mngbangun & Patrick Pillah[1]

Introduction

Young people today live in a complex world with multiple challenges. In Tivland, as it is the case in most of Africa, politics of exclusion, patriarchal socialisation, and some forms of religion have continued to be instruments of oppression of the youth along with women.[2] These constitute, among others, the ideology of the society, which is a superstructure on the socio-economic foundation of any class society.

---

1 Fr Richard Mngbangun, a priest of Gboko Diocese, is the administrator of the Cathedral Church of St John the Baptist, Gboko, and a Chaplain to the Catholic Youth Organisation of Nigeria at the Diocesan and Provincial levels. Sir Patrick Pillah, is a Papal Knight of the Catholic Church, and an Assistant Director at the Presidency, Office of the Head of Service of the Federation.

2 Anne Arabome, "Woman, You are Set Free!" Women and Discipleship in the Church"" in *Reconciliation, Justice, and Peace: The Second African Synod,* ed. Agbonkhianmeghe E. Orobator, (New York: Orbis Books, 2011), 119-130. Cf. Ngozi Frances Uti, "Come, Let Us Talk This Over: On the Condition of Women Religious in the Church" in *Reconciliation, Justice, and Peace: The Second African Synod,* 131-142. See Moses A. Iorapuu, *Patriarchal Ideologies and Media Access: How to Overcome Discrimination Against Tiv Women for Sustainable Rural Development promoting people controlled and participatory communities,* (Rome: Salesian Pontifical University, 2012, Doctoral Thesis No. 819).

However, the sustainability of any human endeavour, be it social, economic, political, cultural, or religious, depends on youth participation. Hence the axiom, "youth of today are leaders of tomorrow," emerges, placing the future of any organisation on the shoulders of the youth. This chapter joins the conversation on the arrival of the Catholic faith among the Tiv a hundred years ago by considering the involvement of youth in the life of the Catholic Church and the efforts by the Church to develop youth in Tivland. The chapter will adopt the term "youth" as employed in official Catholic Church documents by the Vatican, ages 16 to 35.

Although there seems to be no standard global definition, a youth could be defined as a person between 16 and 35 years.[3] Africa and the global south have long insisted that youth is not a range of ages but defined by a diversity of culturally defined social processes that mark the transition from child to adult.[4] In this regard, the United Nations opines that:

> Youth is best understood as a period of transition from dependency to adulthood's independence. That is why, as a category, youth is more fluid than other fixed age groups. However, age is the easiest way to define this group, particularly in education and employment, because 'youth' is often referred to as a person between leaving compulsory education and finding their first job.[5]

For statistical purposes, the United Nations defines 'youth' as those persons between the age of 15 and 24 years, without prejudice to other definitions by member states.[6]

---

3 Courtney Mares, "What is a Youth?" A Synod glossary retrieved at https://www.catholicnewsagency.com.cdn on 3/8/2021.

4 Unini Chioma, "Who is a Youth in Nigeria? Why the Definition by the National Policy 2019 is not acceptable" retrieved at https://thenigerialawyer.com on 23/08/2021.

5 Definition of Youth retrieved at https://www.un.org on 23/08/2021.

6 Ibid.

Prior to the emergence of the national youth policy of 2019, the Nigerian national youth policy of 2009 defined youth as between 18-35 years.[7] However, the 2019 national youth policy changed the above classification, indicating youth in Nigeria to be between 18-29 years. This explains why the National Youth Service Corp scheme is limited to graduates under the age of 30 years.[8] This chapter, though, adopts the usage in Vatican documents of ages 16 to 35.

Tiv Society in Brief

The Tiv people inhabit Benue, Plateau, Nasarawa, Cross River, and Taraba States in Nigeria and the south-western province of the Cameroons.[9] The Tiv consider themselves as one giant family that descended from a common ancestor called Tiv.[10] The word Tiv has triple meanings. It denotes the name given to the ethnic or cultural group of people for identity, the language they speak as *Zwa* Tiv and, lastly, the name of their great ancestor from whom the entire people emerged.[11]

Opinions vary among writers as to the original home of the Tiv from which they may have migrated.[12] Most accounts, however, indicate that the Tiv are of Bantu stock and must have had their

7 Unini Chioma, "Who is a Youth in Nigeria?"

8 Ibid.

9 J.D. Ndera, and Wombo Makar: *Historical Reflections on Chieftaincy and Colonial Experience in Tivland* (Zaria: Ahmadu Bello University Press Ltd, 2013), 2.

10 Godwin Nyor Hembe, *J.S Tarka: The Dilemma of Ethnic Minority Politics in Nigeria*, (Makurdi: Aboki Publisher, 2003), 30.

11 Nicholas Adumbu, Religious *and Cultural Conception of Animals in Tiv Society*, (Makurdi: Aboki Publishers, 2021), 6.

12 Shagbaor F. Wegh, *Globalization of Tiv Social and Cultural Values*, (Makurdi: Sellers Academic Press Ltd, 2018), 12.

home somewhere in Central Africa.[13] The linguistic approach to this question attempts to establish a link between the groups by pointing to the similarity of language. Some scholars base their thesis of a Congo origin for the Tiv on a sixty-seven-word list of similarities in syntax and closeness in meaning across several linguistic groups.[14]

Tiv society is organised on a kinship base, and it is divided into lineages based on blood relationships.[15] Therefore, the people are a homogeneous brotherhood sharing a common genealogy right back to the ancestor Tiv, and everyone's position in society is derived from this ability to trace their origins to the progenitor.[16]

The Tiv are the most predominant and homogeneous ethnic group occupying Benue State, constituting two-thirds of the population.[17] Of the twenty-three local government areas in Benue State, Tiv occupies fourteen. They are Gboko, Buruku, Gwer, Gwer West, Katsina-Ala, Konshisha and Logo. The others are Ukum, Kwande, Ushongo, Makurdi, Vandeikya, Tarka and Guma. All these local government areas before 2012 were a part of the Catholic Diocese of Makurdi. Today, the Catholic Church in Tivland comprises three dioceses of Makurdi, Gboko, and Katsina-Ala. Typical of the continent of Africa as a young continent, the Tiv population is heavily young with the attendant challenges young people encounter, including unemployment and political exclusion across Africa and beyond.

---

13 Ibid.

14 Ibid.

15 T. Wuam, *Moses Orshio Adasu: Religion, Politics, and Development,* (Makurdi: Aboki Publishers, 2004), 6.

16 Ibid.

17 Tarn and, T. *Ya Na Angbian: The Principle, Practice and Relevance in Contemporary Tiv Society*, (Makurdi: Selfers Academic Press Ltd, 2015), 7.

Youth unemployment is a growing problem with significant long-term consequences for individuals, communities, economies, and societies. The transition of young Tiv people from school to work has become longer, more complex and more turbulent. The proportion of young Tiv people searching for jobs has remained at its crisis peak in the last three decades. Underemployment and unemployment have stood out as the greatest challenges plaguing Tiv youth, second only to poverty which keeps a good number out of school in the first place. Where does the Catholic Church feature in this situation?

The Catholic Church and Youth Development in Tivland

Education was a significant tool and entry point of the Catholic Church into Tivland. This was in keeping with the main objectives of missionary activities to cater to the spiritual and material welfare of the people they convert to Christ.[18] With Western education, the people could find both government and church jobs quickly.[19] Consequently, much Christian Religious Instruction (C.R.I.) classes and primary schools were established all over the parishes of the dioceses and prefectures in the North.[20] Tesemchi Makar highlights that "their emphasis, therefore, was on the opening up of primary schools where the pupils were assiduously made to assimilate Catholic doctrines by catechists. The Roman Catholic Mission (RCM) fathers followed this up with visits to the schools and the holding of Mass on Sundays for the adherents."[21]

---

18 J.J. Onutu, "Milestones in the Growth of the Catholic Church in Northern Nigeria" in *The History of the Catholic Church in Nigeria*. Makozi A.O and Ojo, G.J.A. Eds. (Ibadan: Macmillan Nigeria Publishers Limited, 1982), 64.

19 Ibid.

20 Ibid.

21 Tesemchi Makar, *A History of Political Change Among the Tiv in the 19th and 20th Centuries*. (Ph. D. Dissertation, ABU, Zaria, 1975), 190.

In 1936, the R.C.M had fifty schools in Benue Province. By 1949 the number had risen to 149. Consequently, there were several Catholic schools in different parts of the Tiv land, including Gboko, in the late 1930s.[22] The Catholic missions established post-primary schools beginning with Mount Saint Michael's Secondary School, Aliade, (which started in Korinya) in 1953, Mount Saint Gabriel's Secondary School, Makurdi, in 1964. While these catered to the educational needs of the boys, the girls were not left out as Sr Joy Abuh explains;

> The year 1959 saw another step taken when the sisters made two new foundations in Tivland Gboko and Makurdi. Once again, the sisters' conviction of the importance of girls' education led to the setting up in Gboko of a girls' senior primary school and a junior day school…with the introduction of the phasing out of girls' primary schools in the early 1960s, and permission was sought to establish the girls' secondary school in the vacated buildings. This was granted, as there were no catholic secondary schools for girls. So Queen of the Rosary Secondary School (QRSS) Gboko came into existence with the opening class of 17 students.[23]

In a determined fashion to employ the education of young people as a tool for development of both the young people themselves and the society at large, the Catholic Church in the old Makurdi Diocese established St Joseph's Technical College, Makurdi, and St Jude's Technical College, Tse-Mker. These colleges of vocational education, were to develop unconventional talents, skills, crafts, to provide self-employment in the face of the long-term consequences of youth unemployment for individuals and the Tiv

---

22 Ibid.

23 Joy Abuh, "The Evangelizing Strides of the Holy Rosary Sisters in Makurdi Diocese" in *Catholic Diocese of Makurdi at 50: A Celebration of Service to Humanity* Shagbaor F. Wegh, Ed. (Makurdi: Sellers Academic Press Ltd. 2010), 50.

economy at large. Recently, the Catholic Diocese of Makurdi has established the *Tomavee Doo Institute* for fashion and design to train young people in tailoring. The Catholic Diocese of Gboko also established the Convent Vocational Institute, Gboko, to train young people, especially girls, in catering and culinary skills, as well as the Center for Music and the Arts, Gboko, where young people are being trained in music and other arts.

While the Catholic Church in Tivland, has indeed, made significant and outstanding strides through its educational institutions for both boys and girls, the current and long-standing economic situation has raised new questions concerning the Church's education and general evangelisation strategy towards self-reliance, and emancipation. Particularly, given that young people who form the greater majority of the Catholic Church's membership in Tivland are among the most vulnerable economic group, the efforts in vocational training and skills acquisition must be deliberately driven towards empowering the youth devoid of profit-making on the part of the Church.

Catholic youth groups have always served as channels of youth participation and development in the Church. In 1985 the Catholic Bishops Conference of Nigeria, CBCN, accredited the Catholic Youth Organisation of Nigeria (CYON) as an umbrella organisation for all Catholic youth. Prior, what existed was known as the Catholic Youth Movement (C.Y.M.), which was introduced in the old Makurdi Diocese by Achia Dulla and Eunice Awashima Kukwagh, all from St Thomas Parish, Gboko- South, in 1982. The first diocesan president was Godwin Iortim-Uba.

Through the CYON, some young people have discerned for the priesthood and the religious life. CYON periodically organises programs and activities like seminars, drama, debate, quiz competitions on the Church's doctrines, symposia, and others to educate, enlighten, spiritually nourish, and entertain members and the church communities. Among the Tiv, the CYON has been a medium for social engagement of the youth, occupying otherwise idle youth in the villages and forestalling their involvement in social vices.

Besides the CYON, the other organisation that serves as a springboard for youth involvement and their development by the Catholic Church is the Young Catholic Students of Nigeria (YCSN). Through the YCSN, Tarsoo Ade rose through the ranks to become the national president of YCSN and culminated as the international coordinator, headquartered in Paris, France. Papal knight Sir Patrick Pilllah and Lady Victoria Pillah met each other through the YCSN and are a model Catholic family. There are many other examples of such great men and women. Ultimately, the CYON and YCSN have remained veritable tools for Tiv youth involvement in the life of the Catholic Church and the development of these youth in spiritual, social, and intellectual spheres of life.

A remarkable area of youth participation in the life of the Church is their contribution to the infrastructural development efforts of the Church. Despite their financial lack, an appreciable amount of physical for most Church projects like the construction of a new church, priests' residences, church halls and schools, come from the voluntary work of Catholic youth in various parishes across Tivland. For instance, parish youth volunteered most of the skilled, professional, and unskilled in constructing the three recently dedicated Parish Church buildings in the Catholic Diocese of Gboko: St Anne's, Adikpo, Regina Caeli, Akile, and Holy Trinity, Dagba.

Interestingly, today the mega Catholic Youth Centre parish in Makurdi, Catholic Diocese of Makurdi, is built on a piece of land acquired by the Catholic Youth Organisation of Nigeria of the then Makurdi Diocese as the center for youth activities in the diocese. An outstanding question is how the Catholic Church will adapt its strategies for youth development to the turbulent economies and fast-changing political and social structures which currently bear heavily on Tiv youth.

Proposals for better engagement and Development of Tiv Catholic Youth

Pope Francis recently convoked the XV Ordinary General Assembly of the Synod of Bishops, which held from October 3- 28, 2018, under the theme "Young People, The Faith and Vocational Discernment", to address the specific challenges that confront young people in their lives of faith as Catholics. The Synod was a conscious invitation to the Catholic Church and all its members to pay closer attention to young people, taking their questions seriously, patiently walking with them and offering guidance as they discern the best way to live their faith.[24]

Tiv Catholic youth are not exempt from the overall challenges that confront the youth. They particularly share in the specific tensions engulfing Tivland and, by extension, the entire Nigerian society. The near-collapse of security apparatus and apparatchiks, the excruciating poverty, the biting economic situation, the levels of underemployment and unemployment, the uncertainties of political activities, and the collapse of social and moral values all affect youth in Tivland, including Catholics. This calls for more pointed ways of engaging and developing the youth by the Catholic Church in Tivland and beyond.

The youth in Tivland, just as women, belong to the class of the excluded. A consequence of unemployment and biting poverty for many Tiv youth has been the youth's entrenchment of thuggery in the service of politicians, creating a general atmosphere of violence across Tivland. Tiv politicians employ the services of the

---

[24] Synod18 – Documento finale e Votazioni del Documento finale del Sinodo dei Vescovi al Santo Padre Francesco (27 ottobre 2018). Accessed November 9, 2018 at http://press.vatican.va. Cf. Cindy Wooden, "Synod Document: Listen to, Support and Include Young People," *Catholic New Service* http://www.catholicnews.com/services/englishnews/2018/listening-church-pope-gives-new-vision-for-synod-of-bishops.cfm accessed November 8, 2018.

youth against opponents and enemies to secure victory at the polls. Dangerous weapons are left in the hands of the youth, and when elections are over and the politicians disappear, the abandoned youth resort to other criminal activities for survival.

The protracted restiveness in the Sankara axis and fighting in Konshisha, Kwande, Gwer, and most parts of Tivland lends credence to this phenomenon. The Catholic Church will have to sustain the current efforts of engaging the youth positively by keeping them busy and developing them into self-reliant people who contribute to the development of society. While the recent efforts by the Church, including holding consultative sessions with youth in times of crisis, and the renovation of the Akume Atongo Stadium in Katsina-Ala, and the JS Tarka Stadium in Gboko are impressively commendable, efforts at skills acquisition and economic empowerment are indispensable in the current economic situation of Tivland. If this is not addressed, besides youth involvement in dangerous and destructive lifestyles, the Catholic Church will continue to lose numerous youth to the Pentecostal churches.

Clement Terseer Iorliam has offered practical suggestions for developing new ways to engage youth in a typical parish setting.[25] Insisting that one cannot evangelise the youth without understanding their social context, Iorliam calls for the formation of youth pastoral teams in parishes, creating social groups to nurture the faith of young people through social interaction. By recognising

---

[25] Clement Terseer Iorliam, "The Youth in Ministry" in *Practical Ways of Engaging the Laity in Nigeria.* Daniel Ude Asue Ed. (Iperu Remo, Ogun State: Ambassador Publications, 2016), 85-94.

and using the talents of youth in the parish community, they will be creating youth ministries to provide for their unique needs and catechesis.[26]

It is crucially vital to amplify Iorliam's voice, particularly regarding creating Church-based ministries and parachurch ministries to attend to the pressing challenges of youth in the Catholic Church since many of them are leaving for the Pentecostal churches. An excellent example of a parachurch ministry that can be beneficial for youth in Tivland could be extra-mural classes for secondary school students struggling to write qualifying examinations like WASCE and NECO, as well as JAMB.

Vocational training, like basic computer literacy programs and other survival skills like carpentry and tailoring, could be adopted as parish youth ministries to develop young Catholics in the parishes. In doing this, Church authorities must not use such avenues as money-making ventures for the parish but rather with the deliberate intent to develop these youth who give so much to the Church in their time and energies.

Conclusion

The chapter has critically examined various ways in which the Catholic youth in Tivland have contributed to the Church's development. It has also looked at the general problems of the youth in society and the Church. As a way forward, we invite the various

[26] Ibid. 92-93.

hierarchies of the Church to intensify the attention given to young people. If we have hopeless youth in the Church, it is a clear indication that the Church's hope in Tivland is dim.

Like the final document of the XV Ordinary General Assembly of the Synod of Bishops noted, there is the common experience where young volunteers are met by priests and other adults who doubt their commitment or competence and thus are unwilling to share responsibility with them. This attitude has been responsible for the exit of many young people from the Catholic Church in search of places where they feel included and appreciated, like the Pentecostal churches.

Chapter Twelve

The Catholic Church and Pentecostal Presence in Tivland

Gabriel T. Wankar[1]

Introduction

Pentecostalism is believed to be the second-largest Christian denomination worldwide today, second only to Roman Catholicism.[2] Wherever it has appeared, including among the Tiv, the Pentecostal movement emphasises the power of the Spirit to infuse life and the ability of the living presence of Jesus Christ to save from sin and evil. Possession of the Holy Spirit, emphasising direct divine communication, becomes central to religious experience, invoking healing and deliverance from witches, curses, and poverty.

Pentecostalism is often viewed within Catholic circles as proposing solutions that are generally too simple and short-term – for example instant healing, deliverance from forces of evil, and an

1 Fr Gabriel T. Wankar (M.Sc. Development Studies, M. Th. Ecclesiology, S.T.L. Systematic Theology, PhD Systematic Theology) served as Director of Communications for the Catholic Diocese of Makurdi, and a secretary to the Benue State chapter of the Christian Association of Nigeria, (CAN). He is currently assigned in the Archdiocese of San Francisco, California.

2 Cletus C. Gotan, "The Effects of Pentecostalism and Prosperity gospel in Nigeria" in *Jos Studies*: June 2014/22 (Jos: St Augustine Major Seminary, Jos), 25.

increase in material prosperity – for complex questions of human existence. Poverty and the failure of the State in Tivland and beyond to provide viable means of sustenance has led to a significant embrace of the Pentecostal movement by many in the hope of opportunities for a better life.[3] This chapter briefly explores this religious phenomenon to understand the underlying causes of its appeal, especially to the youth in Tivland, besides the common claims of liveliness, deliverance and healing.

Historical Origins and Features of Pentecostalism

The initial term used in connection with this phenomenon was "Pentecostalism," or "Neopentecostalism" and had Protestant roots.[4] With the spiritual reawakening within the Catholic Church occasioned by the Second Vatican Council, Catholic circles saw this term raising doubts because of the Protestant movement that bore the same name. Catholics began to speak of the "Charismatic Renewal" or "Renewal in the Holy Spirit" or "Life in the Spirit." While English-speaking countries seem to have opted for "Catholic Charismatic Renewal," Europeans in the movement seem to prefer "Renewal in the Holy Spirit." Both within and outside the Catholic Church, the phenomenon refers to a blossoming of the Spirit's gifts for a spiritual reawakening in the whole church.

---

3 Gabriel T. Wankar, "What (if anything) can the Catholic Church in Africa learn from Pentecostal/Charismatic Christianity" in *Jos Studies*: June 2014/22 (Jos: St. Augustine Major Seminary, Jos), 63-85. This chapter develops the thoughts expressed in the earlier work. Cf. Clement T. Iorliam, "The Youth in Ministry" in Daniel U. Asue, ed. *Practical Ways of Engaging the Laity in Nigeria* (Iperu Remo: The Ambassador Publications, 2016), 90.

4 Cf. Joseph Boenzi, *Church on the Move: Applied Ecclesiology.* (Unpublished Notes for Ecclesiology and Spiritual Theology Course STSP 4725, Berkeley, September 2011), 151-173.

According to Walter J. Hollenweger, the most crucial root of the Pentecostal movement is a revival in a Black church on Azusa Street in Los Angeles under the leadership of William J. Seymour in 1906.[5] From Los Angeles, this revival spread worldwide – first to predominantly Protestant countries, notably the American South – and then to countries stamped by Catholic culture and other Third World countries, with massive revivals in places like Chile, Korea, and India. These revivals were built on the tradition of the Holiness preachers, who were the first to help the Black slaves escape from their masters, giving people a face, dignity, and independence – one factor that accounts for the enthusiastic adoption that greeted its arrival. These revivals were stamped by oral culture, taken over from the African legacy of the Black slaves, joined in fellowship experienced by songs and prayer.

Prayer meetings are at the heart of the Pentecostal movement, where the exercise of charisms is manifested. The charisms designate personal gifts of the Holy Spirit mentioned by Paul in 1 Corinthians 12:8-10: the gifts of healing, the working of miracles, prophecy, discernment of spirits, speaking in tongues, and the interpretation of what has been spoken in tongues, as examples of such charisms. So also is baptism in the Spirit, which for them has its origin from the words of Christ just before His ascension in Acts 1:5: "John baptised with water, but before many days you shall be baptised with the Holy Spirit." Thus, the baptism in the Holy Spirit is substantially that which happened to the 120 disciples when the Holy Spirit descended on them on the first Pentecost. From the renewal of this same experience, the Pentecostal movement gets both its name and its dynamism.

---

5 Walter J. Hollenweger, *Pentecostalism: Origins and Developments Worldwide* (Massachusetts: Hendrickson Publishers, 2005), 20.

The Faces of African Pentecostalism[6]

Pentecostalism, although a worldwide phenomenon today, is characterized by a giddying diversity from place to place. In Africa, Pentecostalism was preceded by the work of several indigenous prophets who led revivals across the continent from the early years of the twentieth century. Such prophets included William Wade Harris, a Kru man from Liberia who worked in Ghana, and La Cote D' Ivoire, Garrick Sokari Braide of the Niger Delta in Nigeria. Others included Joseph Babalola, also of Nigeria, Simon Kimbangu of the Congo, Isaiah Shembe of South Africa.[7] Most of these prophets did not found churches, as such. Nevertheless, their revivals led to the rise of what became known in South Africa as Zionist churches, in Ghana as Spiritual churches, and Nigeria as *Aladura*, that is, "praying churches." These are churches that are known in the literature as "African independent" or "African initiated" churches (AICs).

I have drawn on the works of Ludovic Lado and J. Kwabena Asamoah- Gyadu to highlight four variants of African Pentecostalism: the independent African churches with Pentecostal features (also called "spiritual churches"), the classic Pentecostal churches (dependent or independent), the neo-Pentecostal churches and the charismatic movements within the Catholic or Protestant churches. The independent African churches with Pentecostal features are the oldest variants on the continent, first appearing in South Africa, where the activities of the American John G. Lake (1908-

---

6 See Gabriel T. Wankar, *Towards the New Evangelisation: Lessons from Pentecostal/ Charismatic Christianity to the Catholic Church in Africa* (San Diego: CreateSpace Independent Publishing Platform, 2013), 9ff.

7 Ludovic Lado, "African Catholicism in the face of Pentecostalism," translated by Paul Burns, in *African Christianities, Concilium*: 2006/4, edited by Eloi Messi Metogo (London: SCM, Cantebury Press Ltd), 23-24.

1912) produced such churches as the Apostolic Faith Mission (the White branch) and Zion Christian Church (the Black branch).

According to Ludo, it was from this missionary root that South African Zionism sprang, and it would be safe to include well-known independent African churches that date from the colonial period like Kimbaguism in Congo (1921), the Aladura Church in Nigeria (1930), Alice Lenshina's Lumpa Church in Zambia (1995) in the category of independent African churches with Pentecostal features.[8] The independent African churches aimed at restoring to the African church the vitality of the presence of the Holy Spirit, the lack of which was seen as accounting for the "dry denominationalism" of the older historical churches.

Classic Pentecostal churches, on their part, include all those churches with North American roots under the influence of the pioneers of the Pentecostal renewal of the last century (Charles Parham and William J. Seymour) that spread to parts of the world, naturally including Africa. One of their fastest-growing congregations, the Assemblies of God Church, founded in the United States in 1914, began its missionary activities in Africa in the 1920s – first in English-speaking countries and then spreading to French-speaking countries. These churches followed the same *modus operandi* as that adopted by missionary movements for evangelising bordering countries through building networks on a regional scale. In Ghana, for example, the largest Pentecostal church in this category today is the Church of the Pentecost, founded there in 1953 by the Scottish pastor James McKeown. Others in this category would

8 Wankar, "What (if anything) can the Catholic Church in Africa learn from Pentecostal/Charismatic Christianity" 69. All of these churches were found by people indigenous to those countries, undoubtedly charismatic figures, who claimed to be inspired by God or the Holy Spirit for a special mission, particularly of healing and leading a crusade against witchcraft and other traditional practices.

include the church of the Four Square Gospel, Apostolic Faith Mission, and Elim Pentecostal – all established in Africa through missionary activities of North American and Western European Pentecostals.

The next variant, the neo-Pentecostal churches, were the fruit of the Pentecostal renewal of the 1960s and 1970s. Despite their fundamental adoption of the essence of classic Pentecostal teaching, a few things distinguish them: the importance of the theology of material prosperity, display of pastors' wealth, paying of tithes, employing the media as a means of evangelising, and hyper emphasis on healing rituals. David O. Oyedepo's Winner's Chapel is a typical example of churches in this category. Founded in the Lagos city of Nigeria in 1983, it has several branches today, both within Africa and beyond. Other names within this category include Mensa Otabil of the International Central Gospel Church in Ghana and Andrew Wutawanashe of the Family of God in Zimbabwe. Its theology of material prosperity[9] as a sign of divine blessing attracts entrepreneurs and the teeming, jobless young people searching for opportunities. The Winner's Chapel is a typical neo-Pentecostal church to be found across Tivland.

The fourth variant of Pentecostalism in Africa, the charismatic renewal movements and trans-denominational fellowships, is composed of both Catholics and Protestants in their membership. They undoubtedly spring from the influence of the recent movement of

9 According to this theology, the life of abundance that flows from Jesus' victory over sin and death is concerned not with the next life but with life here on earth; it is demonstrated by wealth, health, prestige, prosperity. The obligation to pay tithes here operates on a prevailing logic by which God will generously reward those who give generously to the church or the pastor in return. So the rich give generously in the hope of seeing their businesses prosper; the poor, for their part, deprive themselves for the pastor in the hope of receiving a hundredfold from the little they have. This religious ideology of prosperity, bitterly criticized by the older churches, has led to the rapid enrichment of the pastors of some of these new structures.

Pentecostal revival on the older historic churches, including the Catholic Church. The charismatic renewal groups usually function within existing mainline denominations in order to help renew them from within. Their main emphases are Bible study, prayer, and the integration of charismatic renewal phenomena into mainline-church Christianity. Born entirely out of lay initiative, these movements aim to integrate renewal phenomena within existing mainline denominations to renew them from within. The trans-denominational fellowships are like the charismatic renewal groups, but they exist outside the boundaries of denominationalism and provide space for like-minded believers with shared experiences of the Spirit to fellowship outside church control.

Prominent in this category are the Full Gospel Businessmen's Fellowship International, Women Aglow, and Intercessors for Africa. These movements implanted in different nations of Africa in various ways. In Nigeria, for example, the university campuses provided the nuclei for the expansion of the charismatic movements in the 1970s, and this has also become a common phenomenon in all University campuses in Tivland to date. Mega Pentecostal churches are to be found very near the university campuses in Tivland: The Mountain of Fire and Miracles is found very near University of Agriculture Makurdi and the Winners Chapel is to be found outside the First Gate of the Benue State University, and Dunamis is found just outside the Second Gate. These are very strategic and calculative locations.

Pentecostal Presence Among the Tiv

The arrival of Pentecostalism in Tivland followed the same pattern as other parts of Africa, where it was preceded by the work of indigenous prophets who led revivals across the continent. Peter Ichull attributes spiritual growth and incursion of the Pentecostal faith in Tivland following Catholics and evangelicals, to the two significant pioneers and televangelists John Ornguze and Joe

Ichull.[10] In the early seventies, he holds that many Ibos with deep emotional scars of the Nigerian civil war found consolation in the wave of Christian revivals that enveloped Southern Nigeria after the war. Some prominent Ibo preachers also left their land to retail the good news to their brethren scattered in diaspora, which will account for the presence of the movement in Tivland. "In Benue, brother Chuks of Scripture Union, William Okoye of Freedom in Christ, and Nzuko of Light of Life had made significant inroads into Makurdi and Gboko. Though the target of these new churches was Ibos, the environment began to feel the collateral impact of their 'spiritual invasion.'"[11]

According to Ichull, although younger people like Tor Uja, Emma Maker, Godwin Ikyernum, Sister Dooshima Angira-Ornguze, William Bendega, and Peter Ichull embraced the movement since 1975, with Pius Dyegeh also coming on board after retiring from the Police in 1977, the bang came with the trio of Joe Ichull, John Ornguze, and Mike Dzuamo. The decision of these old friends who had received Christ at different locations to share their testimonies with residents of Gboko marked the tipping point of Pentecostal revival in the town.[12] Just before their arrival, Mike Jerusalem Dzuamo had already taken up an appointment with Gboko Christian Youth Center as a director while serving as a member of the Free Life Team, run by Peter Dzawua, who was not yet a Pentecostal preacher.

In 1978, Mike Dzuamo put together a meeting in Gboko that would become the platform upon which John Ornguze would un-

10 Peter Ichull, "Benue Pentecostal revival of the 1970s: A Tribute to Rev. John T. Ornguze." (An unpublished Funeral Oration).

11 Peter Ichull, "Benue Pentecostal revival of the 1970s: A Tribute to Rev. John T. Ornguze." (An unpublished Funeral Oration).

12 Peter Ichull, "Benue Pentecostal revival of the 1970s: A Tribute to Rev. John T. Ornguze." (An unpublished Funeral Oration).

veil the Lord's vision. Joe Ichull would soon join the team, and their preaching programs would cause many of the schools in Gboko to virtually shut down as students violated every rule to attend the meetings. The students, in turn, took the good news to fellow students, their teachers, and parents, with spiral effects across households, churches, and denominations. This marked Pentecostal origins in Gboko and its spread across all of Benue, including into Idoma and Igede lands. Prominent among the movement's early success were Pastors Paul Aule, Isaac Tsughum, and Paul Enenche.

The second wave of the Pentecostal arrival among the Tiv was the launching of Rev. John's Ornguze'e TV program "Jesus is the answer."[13] This program allowed families to listen to the Gospel from Rev. John. His diction and American accent were the hooks that pegged the Benue youth to the program and the messages. The launching of the media outreach came with the establishment of the Christian Center, which served as a hub to train other evangelists through Bible study and planting of local churches to keep the coals hot and burning with the Gospel.

Equally worthy of mention is Brother Gbile Akani, who had a robust Baptist origin. He had come to Gboko in 1979 as a Youth Corp member and was teaching physics and stayed back after his service. His evangelical work soon became a phenomenon that would lead to the establishment of Peace House in Gboko. The organisation has become an international hub for Christian discipleship for all denominations. Pentecostal denominations to be found in Tiv villages today include, the Assemblies of God Church, the church of the Four Square Gospel, Apostolic Faith Mission, Winner's Chapel, Living Faith, All Nations Evangelism Ministry, among others. Recent entrants to the stage with reasonable follow-

13 Peter Ichull, "Benue Pentecostal revival of the 1970s: A Tribute to Rev. John T. Ornguze." (An unpublished Funeral Oration).

ing, include, Pastor Tom Ingya, Evangelist Sam Zuga, and Prophet Saint Treasure Ayem. All of these preachers, besides the different programs they are involved in, offer material support and opportunities to youth who are socially disposed, which explains the attraction of the youth to them.

The Challenge of Pentecostalism and Possible Lessons to be learned

Like any living organism, the Catholic Church, too, has had to react over time to the internal and external demands made on it – in other words, to redefine itself in the human context of its time. I have argued that the Tiv Christians, including Catholics of the post-independence years, have found themselves struggling in a society with wars, internally displaced people, droughts, famines, migration, poverty, the scourge of HIV/AIDS, and a failed State. There is a deep sense of insecurity and frustration at the thwarting of legitimate aspirations. While many people are genuinely moved by the Spirit to some religious experience, numerous instances of the mass movement of young people from the Catholic Church and other older denominations to embrace the Pentecostal movement could be attributed to numerous other factors.

These include disagreements and disappointment with church leadership, leadership tussles and issues bothering on sustenance and economic survival.[14] Notwithstanding, I propose that the Catholic Church in Tivland take a look at some of the approaches of Pentecostal/Charismatic Christianity in responding to certain pastoral issues, especially those that do not bother on the celebration of the sacraments.

---

14 This is a development of my views on the subject matter. I have found through further research that poverty largely accounts for the pull to new churches, especially in poorer nations like Nigeria with a failed state and crumbling economy.

Role of the Laity/Lay Leadership

The ecclesiology of the Pentecostal/Charismatic tradition follows the New Testament principle, particularly evident in Pauline writings; that participating in Christ is like functioning as members of the human body. Each part has, by definition, a function within the body, hence the reference to the believing community as the "Body of Christ" (1 Cor 12:12-31). The *charismata* or "gifts of grace," as exercised by an individual or groups of believers, constitute their "ministry." The different ministries are coordinated within the local church to make it charismatically functional.

Also, in the wake of life's challenges, Pentecostals appear to offer human warmth; care and support in small and close-knit communities; sharing of purpose and fellowship; attention for the individual; protection, and security; especially in crises such as loss of a job, sickness, and loss of dear ones; reconciliation and rehabilitation of marginalised individuals; e.g., the divorced, widows, immigrants and the like.

Though there may be the need to renew and refocus existing forms of lay associations and ministries in the Catholic Church in Tivland, I maintain that some underlying and encompassing factors for the pull to Pentecostal churches seems more economic in nature. The dice of development is heavily loaded against Tivland. Despite its favourable agricultural environment, the present attacks on farmers and the neglect from the government is compounding poverty in Tivland and may linger for a while. To be able to impact the lives of its members in the current circumstances requires the Catholic Church to increase its tempo in agro-allied industries. The development in farming and industrial processing of agricultural products will be crucial, not only to turn the huge annual wastages into profit ventures, but most importantly to offer job opportunities to the many jobless youth in Tivland.

Youth Empowerment/Development

The most significant appeal of Pentecostalism in most African countries in the recent past is the attention given to the youth. Many universities are turning out graduates every year with no business and job opportunities available to them. Political leadership requires party membership and money that is not within reach of these youth. The various youth programs of the Pentecostal movement, the identification of talents, abilities, and achievements where individuals could even rise to leadership and authority is much cherished by the youth.

Pentecostal/Charismatic ministries have several social functions uniquely integrated with the religious function due to the adversity in the social environment, especially for the youth, which reinforces my economic leitmotif theses. They have programs geared to skills acquisition and entrepreneur training sessions, as well as leadership development, creating networks for job opportunities to support young people to work their way into public office and influence the agenda of the state. Architect Nguvan Kyenge has, in the last few years, initiated Coaching series and Business/Vocational training in Makurdi metropolis, which she integrates with the All Nations Evangelism Ministry programs. The Catholic Church in Tivland will need to borrow a leaf from such initiatives, not just content with offering moral lessons to the youth but creating opportunities for economic enhancement.

African Worldview/Inculturation

Essential elements in African religiosity, including the Tiv, are encounters with the spiritual world: as malevolent powers seeking to destroy people, marine spirits negating efforts at public morality, or as the performance of ritual in order to solicit help from the powers of beneficence. Besides, over the years, the HIV/AIDS scourge and other forms of disease have been commonplace in Africa amidst abject poverty. With no financial capacity to seek orthodox medication, Pentecostal healing crusades and miracles seemingly appeal to people in need of healing.

A few Tiv Catholic priests have embraced the "healing ministry," including the late Fr Christopher Utov, Fr Hyacinth Alia, late Fr Stephen Suega, Fr Emmanuel Agundo, CSSP., Fr Kenneth Koughna, CSSP., Fr Matthew Dzer, Fr Emmanuel Asue, Fr Julius Agah, Fr Emmanuel Mngbakpa, employing many of the tools of Pentecostalism in their ministry. However, all the sacraments of the Catholic Church are healing by nature, and the recent huge massive embrace of the Tridentine Mass by young people is a counter indication to the viability of diluting Catholic liturgical celebrations with Pentecostal nuances to win following. People need authentic spiritual nourishment and viable economic means of survival.

The prosperity Gospel is closely related to healing, which promises material prosperity and physical health to those who have sufficient faith in God. In a land of abject poverty, healing and deliverance makes a natural appeal, again bringing us back to the economic undertones of the pull to miracle centers. In the developed nations of the world, people do not run from church to church in search of miracles, since they have the structures and means of survival. Economic empowerment should become a conscious evangelising tool for the Catholic Church in Tivland, in the same fashion as education and healthcare have been over the last hundred years.

Conclusion

Many writers, including Catholic theologians, have wrongly proposed the very well-known "progressive" (Culture of Death) strategy of gradualism, or incrementalism, as a solution towards saving the Catholic Church from losing its members to other churches.[15] This "progressive" ploy, couched in the language of "reading the signs of the times," employs the strategy of going one step at a time and let people get used to it before moving on. This has been done all over the world, the obvious example being abortion.[16] First, to save the mother's life, then wait a year or two, then for the rape or incest of the mother, then wait a while, then abortion for fetal birth defects, then another two or three years, then abortion for the mother's health, and before you know what has happened, you have abortion on demand today. This is the well-known "progressive" strategy of gradualism, or incrementalism, used to avoid pushback.

Gradualism has impacted the history of the "mainline" Protestant churches, especially in the United States (Methodist, Presbyterian, United Church of Christ, Episcopalian), where these progressive forces have pushed them to crisis. These churches noticed their declining membership in the 1960s and decided that the problem was **not** that their theology and practice was getting looser and looser, but that they needed more women in ministry. So soon they had "priestesses" and "pastorettes," and after this even "bishopettes." The result was a catastrophe. Millions left these churches, and their membership plunged by half.

The solution to the pull of members to other churches, especially Pentecostalism, as history has shown us, is not destroying Catholic doctrine, theology, liturgy, nor ordaining homosexual and married men and women, but to hold firm to our theology, which

---

15 In an earlier work, Wankar, *Towards the New Evangelisation: Lessons from Pentecostal/Charismatic Christianity to the Catholic Church in Africa,* I blindly adopted this view, which I now denounce based on further research and the development of my thoughts on the subject.

16 Cf. Brian Clowes, "Nigeria Stands Strong," in *The Wanderer* Vol. 146. No. 25. June 2013, 1-2; *The Facts of Life: An Authoritative Guide to Life and Family issues* (2nd Ed. Minneapolis: Human Life International, 2001).

has endured and survived worse attacks from the past centuries to this day. The basic lesson to learn is to incorporate an economic enhancement approach to its evangelisation strategy in Tivland. This will involve, as noted earlier, scaling up development in farming and industrial processing of agricultural products, not only to turn the huge annual wastages into profit ventures, but most importantly to offer job opportunities to the many jobless youth in Tivland.

Chapter Thirteen

A Century of the Catholic Church in Tivland: An Anglican Bishop's Perspective

Nathan Nyitar Inyom[1]

A journey of a century is indeed a long journey. Imagining this journey from the mirror of a traveller on the Nigerian roads, it would be no gainsaying that the travellers must have travelled through uncharted roads, climbed mountains and valleys, gone through muddy waters, and experienced all the mayhem that characterized journeys on Nigerian roads. Today, it is even worse that besides the no palatability of the roads, the recklessness of commercial drivers, which have been responsible for many road accidents, you have to face robbery and extortions from both men of the underworld and uniformed men who are paid to keep the roads secured. One also needs to pray not to fall into the hands of kidnappers. When loved ones take off on a journey today, one is anxious and restless until you hear that they have arrived safely. It is common now that people give testimonies and offer thanksgivings in Churches for safe trips.

In the same vein, one could rightly imagine that the Catholic Church's journey of a century in Tivland has been a voyage full of experiences of the good, the bad, and the ugly. Nevertheless, the Church has sailed through these one hundred years, and it is

1 The Rt Rev. (Dr) N. N. Inyom, (GJP), is the Bishop of the Anglican Diocese of Makurdi in Benue State, Nigeria.

indeed worth giving thanks to God. Therefore, I join the Catholic faithful and the Christian communities worldwide to felicitate with the Catholic Church for this milestone of achieving a hundred years in Tivland.

Not many people have been around in the last one hundred years to comment about the emergence and growth of the Catholic Church in Tivland in the period, but documents and landmark achievements are there to tell the story. As a Bishop of the Anglican Church in Benue and the oldest in this land, I have had a close working relationship with the Catholic Church. The first indigenous Bishop of the Catholic Diocese of Makurdi, Most Rev. Athanasius A. Usuh (now deceased), was a close friend in ministry. We shared ideas, and I learned a lot from him. Moreover, from hindsight, I would like to say that the Catholic Church in Tivland has had tremendous and undeniable impact on Christianity in Tivland. The Catholic Church is a model for all churches in faith, evangelism, worship, and practices. I want to comment on a few of these outstanding achievements of the Catholic Church.

First, the Catholic Church has had great evangelical strides in Benue and Tivland. The principal mandate of the Church is to spread the gospel, plant churches for worship, and the discipleship of her members, in order to fulfill the Great Commission.[2] This mandate is observed to be the soul of the Catholic Church. The Church, which started possibly with a family, grew to a congregation, has grown and spread all over places within and outside the bounds of Benue. From the seed of the gospel the Catholic Church planted in Tivland, a hundred years ago, and sixty years after creating the Catholic Diocese of Makurdi, other Dioceses of Lafia (Nassarawa State), Otukpo, Katsina-Ala, and Gboko have also been created. The Catholic Church is in every nook and cran-

2 Matthew 28: 18 – 20.

nies of Tivland and the Benue Valley at large. This passion for the spread of the gospel and the planting of Churches is commendable. In addition, and alongside these Churches built across Tivland, the Catholic Church has also established schools and hospitals that provide quality education and job opportunities to Benue people.

Secondly, the leadership of the Church has been able to indigenise the Catholic Church in Tivland. It is a popular mission paradigm that the gospel and the Church must be contextualised wherever it is established to be relevant and address the needs of the people where it is domiciled. Most Western missionary efforts in Africa in the early nineteenth century could not make much impact because they were 'foreign' and 'western' in their approaches.[3]

For the early Catholic Missions, it is particularly noted that 'there were no early steps for indigenisation of Christianity, Church buildings were Western; hymns were of Western words and tunes, and the liturgy of Western style. Worst of all, some Roman Catholic Missions insisted that the Mass be said in Latin. Even when they began to recruit indigenes for the priesthood, they were to study in Latin.'[4] For this reason, Neil observes that "one of the gravest weaknesses of Roman Catholicism in India was its extreme foreignness …."[5] It, therefore, became expedient that going forward, the Church must contextualise her missions. One of the commendable and favourable approaches to contextualisation has been 'indigenisation.'[6]

---

3 See J. Herbert Kane, *A Concise History of the Christian World Mission: A Panoramic View of Mission from the Pentecost to the Present*. (Grand Rapids: Baker Book House, 1980), 163 and Alec R. Vidler, *The Church in an Age of Revolution* (London: Penguin Books, 1974), 252._

4 Godwin T. Simon, *The Church in Holistic Mission. (*Kaduna: M.O. Press, 2008), 87.

5 Stephen Neil, *A History of Christian Missions*. (New York: Penguin, 1964), 406.

6 A Neely, "What is a Context and what is Contextualization?" in *Christian Mission: A*

The Catholic Church in Tivland has duly utilised making the Church native wherever it is planted. While many Churches and Missions in Tivland are still perceived as 'foreign,' it is not so with the Catholic Church. The Tiv people see the Church as native to them. The Catholic Church has its liturgy, hymns and songs, and many kinds of literature in Tiv language. The priests are mainly indigenous and also trained to use the Tiv language in their homilies. This is highly commendable, and I think it has been primarily responsible for the Catholic Church's acceptance in Tivland.

Thirdly, given my long years of stay and ministry in this land (I have been a Priest for 37 years and a Bishop for 29 years), I have watched many ministers and ministries rise and fall. I can say unreservedly that the Catholic Church has been outstanding in the training and discipline of her priests. The Catholic priests are theologically sound and well-behaved. It is a hallmark of ministry, particularly in preaching, that the preacher should 'rightly divide the word of truth.'[7] Unfortunately, today, the pulpit has become an all-comers affair. Untrained people take to the pulpit to preach and teach errors and heresies, and the gullible are falling for it. As ministers of the gospel, we must interpret God's word to his people faithfully. Moreover, to do this, we cannot negate the place of training.

Fourthly, I must acknowledge the role of the Catholic Church in ecumenical activities in this land. The Catholic Church has been in the frontiers of promoting unity amongst Churches in this land. The Church has played vital roles in the leadership of Christian Association of Nigeria (CAN) in Benue and helped in addressing issues of

---

Case Study Approach (Maryknoll: NY: Orbis, 1995), 3 -13 defines indigenisation as the practice of making the Church native wherever it is planted.

7 2 Timothy 2: 15

concern in Benue and for the Tiv people. For example, the Catholic Church stood with other churches to address burial rites in Tivland, which before now had been cumbersome and burdensome.

Finally, I must conclude on a personal note. Like I said earlier, I have enjoyed a close working relationship with the Catholic Church. This was made possible by the love and friendship extended to me by the late Bishop, Most Rev. A. A. Usuh. He was a personal friend. He invited me to Synods and conferences; and shared ministry materials with me. I have many Catholic publications on my shelves, and they are worthwhile. Upon the instruction of the leadership of the Catholic Church, I was admitted and treated for free at St Thomas hospital, Ihugh, and Bishop Murray Hospital, Makurdi. Catholic priests have hosted me in their rectories over the years whenever I went on tour to Anglican Churches with no parsonages. Before the demise of Most Rev. Usuh, he gave out in marriage his niece to one of my priests. For me, this is a clear testament, not just about friendship but also the unity of the body of Christ. Therefore, let this be a challenge to all those who fan embers of denominational differences.

I congratulate and admire the outstanding work of the current Catholic Bishops in Tivland. May I humbly encourage all of them not to abandon the footsteps of the revered father in the faith, Most Revd A. A. Usuh. Let him continue to live on in the examples he has left for all of us. I will never forget the visit of some Catholic Priests with members of CWO. They came to acknowledge and appreciate the friendship between Bishop Usuh and myself, and by extension, between the Catholic Church and the Anglican Church. I pray that God will keep us continually united to expand the gospel of Christ in Tivland.

Once again, congratulations for the centenary celebration of the Catholic Church in Tivland.

CHAPTER FOURTEEN

The Catholic Church and the Future in Tivland: An Elder's Perspective

Shima Gyoh[1]

My earliest memories in Gboko date back to the middle 1940s when my mother used to take me to the Dutch Reformed Church Mission (DRCM) on Sundays. I understood and enjoyed the Tiv church songs composed in the cadence of traditional Tiv music, telling the story of Jesus in the language I understood. One day, she just switched over to the Roman Catholic Church without explanation. I was about seven, brought up in a society that did not encourage children to "query" parents or participate in discussions on serious subjects. The contrast was much. All the priests were white people, services were in Latin, and the hymns, translated into English from the historical collection of church liturgy were sung in monotone. In any case, at this time I did not understand English.

My mother must have noted a drop in her son's enthusiasm, so she gave me a stiff lecture on religion after which the fear of Hell became the dominant factor in my life. I followed her admonitions, attended catechism classes, eventually passed the examination for baptism and became a baptised and regular church goer.

---

1 Shima Gyoh is a renowned surgeon, retired Professor of Surgery at the Benue State University, and Former Permanent Secretary of the Federal Ministry of Health.

It led to my later becoming an altar boy who could sing the entire *Missa de Angelis* from memory, who studied Latin and seriously considered becoming a priest. I fell in love with Latin liturgy, particularly with the sung Mass and, surprisingly I was no longer enthusiastic about its replacement by the new Mass following the Second Vatican Council. This development took place over many years of education, and could not be depended upon for rapid and wide spreading of the messages the Church would want to impart. Many people attended church, but, like me, out of the fear of Hell and the hope for Heaven without a genuine internalisation of the message, i.e. in their daily lives.

The picture has radically changed! One of the outstanding features of the Catholic Church is that its worship, the Mass, is built on a skeleton that gives it its strength and identity. Any changes it undergoes have been so slow and gentle that, should a person from the Middle Ages miraculously walk in today, he would still be at home. The skeleton is supported by decorative branches, so to speak, that vary according to the ecclesiastical year, designed to give meaning to current issues. These branches, together with some parts of the skeleton are now decorated with beautiful plumage in the form of wonderful chants beautifully sung in the Tiv language by highly gifted and well-trained choristers. Though I am now a Quaker, the services strike a deep chord in me. These developments will widen the acceptance and internalisation of Catholic Christianity regardless of the standard that education in Tivland follows in the future.

Indigenisation will need to include the Church illustrations, particularly of the Holy Family. Jesus and Mary are always shown as Caucasians, a practice originated by the Caucasian people of Europe during their own internalisation of the Christian message. We accepted Christianity from Europe together with the packing boxes in which it came. At the time we were not so politically sensitised to racial prejudice perpetrated against non-Caucasians world-wide.

The continued portrayal of the Holy Family as Caucasian is going to become more and more problematic to other races.

In 1964, I was a medical student on clinical attachment to the University Teaching Hospital Ibadan, and I saw, for the first time, in a mural in the Catholic University Chapel, the Holy Family depicted as black Africans. Jesus wore a cloth draped over his left shoulder in the manner of our traditional dress. It was decades ahead of its time and must have been done by an inspired person. I have not seen such portrayal at any other place, but the Church would need to adopt this for the future for two important reasons. First, the Holy Family was not white or Caucasian, and scientific reconstruction from the skulls of the people who lived at that time in Palestine gives Jesus a more African look. Second, it will be an important contribution to the racial equality increasingly being demanded by the people, and among the Tiv it would become less of "*the White man's religion.*"

Then there is the important name issue. As a condition for baptism, you must discard your Tiv name and adopt an "English name," a practice which I could not find in any official Catholic document. I was told that it should be the name of a saint who, together with your guardian angel, would continuously pray for you and reinforce your ability to fight sin. Because baptism is also referred to as christening, and the first "given name" regarded as the one at baptism, Nigerians tend to assume that the first name, the "Christian name," must be an "English" name.

At school, my colleagues would not accept that the cultural name my parents gave me was my "Christian" name. I keep writing "Christian" and "English" as if they were synonymous, but I was not sure some of the foreign names the priests accepted, like Churchill or Chamberlain—adopted from colonial administrators—actually belonged to saints. Besides, a large majority of people came to believe that these names were the proof that one had become a Christian. They resented being addressed by their cultural names. At school, you could start a fight by calling a child by his cultural name. My brother's daughter was refused baptism by a Catholic priest because we had insisted on the use of a Tiv name that was very important to us. Her mother later "smuggled" her (without informing us, as my brother and I used to pull her leg), to be baptised "Rosemary." Although definitely English, we had not seen such a name under the list of saints. Later, parents began to give such names at birth, but we of the old generation were given only Tiv names, and later chose the baptismal names ourselves.

Some children became so enthusiastic that they renounced their Tiv names, contemptuously referring to them as "*ati a Mbatsav*" or witchcraft names. This was regrettable because the Tiv give names with deep philosophical meanings that often indicate personal, family or predominant events. Many, when called along with the father's name, make profound statements. My life is dominated by love for the truth, so I named my daughter, *Mimidoo* (*truth is good*). When joined with my name, it makes a statement which I want the world to know. *Mimidoo Shima*, meaning *Shima loves truth.* My full name is *Orkashima* (man is the heart). "Heart" in the name means "character," as it is assumed to be the center of human emotions. It therefore means "the sum of a man is his character."

A girl might be named *Ngohile* (mother has returned) to celebrate the feeling that the baby is a reincarnation of a dearly loved mother, and *Aondongu* (God exists), is an expression of gratitude, faith or submission. Although many people now retain their cultural names in addition to the new foreign name, most Catholic priests studiously ignore it. Over the years, I have attended scores of christenings, funerals and remembrance Masses during which priests always omitted the cultural name and use only the "English" names taken at baptism and confirmation.

In the early forties, Gboko had only three churches. The DRCM had its headquarters at Mkar and a church in Gboko. With its approach in vernacular, it gave good competition to the other two.

The Anglicans had their Church Missionary Society (CMS) located just after the Prison Warders Barracks, opposite the present Gboko Club. The Roman Catholic Church was first at Agedam, but later moved to where St John's Cathedral of Gboko Diocese currently sits. Each provided primary school education. But I went to Gboko Elementary (now Central) School, run by the Tiv Native Authority—the Local Government at this time of colonial administration.

While education at the other churches stagnated at the primary level, the Catholic Church surged ahead to the secondary school stage. As education became important to the people, so did the Catholic Church. It has produced great men and women in both the secular and the spiritual life of the country. The Catholic Church has a reputation of providing quality education, and has done so both in religious and secular fields. This service will become more important as standards continue to fall in public educational institutions. The university level should be the next obvious target in the not-too-distant future.

The Church's health services have constituted hope for the poorest of the poor, in that they are reputed to welcome even patients unable to pay hospital bills. Maintenance of such institutions would require fund-raising activities in Tivland, as poverty is on the ascendancy due to the poor fiscal policies at both the State and Federal levels. Moreover, the displacement of inhabitants from their villages and farms by Fulani invaders has magnified poverty, and the problem is getting worse. The Church will have an important role to play in the housing, feeding and rehabilitation of these internally displaced people (IDP) presently accommodated in dreadful camps that are not weather-proof. Education of their children is a crucially important problem not being handled by the government. Depression of education will cause unimaginable damage, and the Church can mitigate it by increasing its role in the education of displaced children.

Some moral issues posed difficult problems when the Catholic Church first came to Tivland. Polygamy was an established way of life from time immemorial. When the Catholic Church came, it demanded that the faithful dispose of this cultural baggage. A prominent man and his five wives were all baptised into the Church, but he was barred from taking Communion because he was still "living in sin," unless he took the Sacrament of Holy Matrimony with one of his wives after sending the rest away. The man reasoned that he grew up in a culture where polygamy was proper and married the women when they were young and "marketable," and they had borne children. Their families had become linked to his, and it would be a social abomination to send a wife away when she had not violated any serious social norm. It would cause profound distress to give the impression that they and their children were illegitimate. He quoted the Biblical records where David and Solomon had many wives without one word of reprimand from God, but to no avail.

Industrialisation, mechanisation of farming and education are powerful forces that end polygamy, and neither of these is developing at the rate that would achieve it within one lifetime. Monogamy is now legal for marriages conducted in the Registry and by the Church, making subsequent polygamy an offence. However, the problem still remains, as the occasional polygamist still comes into the Church. Perhaps there might be another way of accommodating them without upsetting the legitimacy of women or their children and without giving the impression that the Church was compromising on the Sacrament of Matrimony.

The ordination of Tiv priests opened a new vista for the congregation. Although many of us were in awe of the priest as our intermediary with God, and were a bit intimidated by the cassock, the profession underwent some demystification when many priests began to dress in ordinary clothes, mixing with us at social occasions, and some exhibiting the same weaknesses as we ordinary folks. Will it be easy to sustain a celibate priesthood among the Tiv in the long run? Since the Church regards celibacy as a discipline, and not a doctrine, it might need to consider married priests in the Tivland of the future if the alternative would be frequent desertion of the cloister for the hearth and the multiple problems it can raise.

The Tiv, like most Nigerians, love brightly coloured uniforms with shiny buttons. The Knights of the Church look flamboyant, but their functions are presently obscure. They seem to many to be an exclusive society for the wealthy—very visible at church on Sundays. They have attracted much admiration and criticism. Perhaps the "order" can be developed as a group of volunteers that assist in the Church's social work, but their bearing is as if they are not the type to "dirty their hands." The congregation needs a better understanding of their function.

The dice of development is heavily loaded against Tivland. Despite its favourable agricultural environment, the present attacks on farmers and neglect from the government will sustain poverty for the foreseeable future. The Catholic Church would not be able to carry out the heavy spiritual and temporal work without a strong financial backbone. It would need to increase its tempo in agro-allied industries, particularly the development in farming and industrial processing of agricultural products, to turn the huge annual wastages into profit ventures. The Church would have to be open on its financial matters so that the people would believe it does not accept favours from those whose wealth stems from obscure or criminal activities.

Afterword

Proposing a Model for Personnel Management Practices and Staff Welfare in Church Institutions for the Government

Gabriel T. Wankar[1]

Two simple reasons account for the initial impulse to undertake this collection of essays to mark the centenary of the encounter of the Tiv people with the Catholic faith. Firstly, to put what little is known of the history and enormous sacrifices of the early missionaries and their collators on record before an entire generation is gone, rendering the recollection of this history hazier, and the task of filling many historical gaps becomes impossible.

Historical accounts of missionary activities in Africa usually mention the expatriate missionary priests and sisters' names and neglect any mention of their lay collators. Many natives supported the missionaries as catechists, interpreters, cooks, mission support staff (who in many cases carried the missionaries on their backs to cross streams and dangerous paths), and others took up roles

---

1 Fr Gabriel T. Wankar (M.Sc. Development Studies, M. Th. Ecclesiology, S.T.L. Systematic Theology, PhD Systematic Theology) served as Director of Communications for the Catholic Diocese of Makurdi, and a secretary to the Benue State chapter of the Christian Association of Nigeria, (CAN). He is currently assigned in the Archdiocese of San Francisco, California.

in the liturgical setting like choir directors, composing songs for worship, while others served as catechism teachers.

In the Korinya area of Tivland, for example, Fr Dominic Jir recalls such pioneers to include Catechists James Azuana Dabo (who was later moved to St John's Gboko), Bonaventure Kange Ode, Patrick Yanyam Iber, Michael Shiko, while Joseph Ajayi Ade was the cook. James Aginde, who started as a mission boy, moved to serve as a steward to Bishop Murray and died while serving Bishop Usuh in the same role in 2003.[2]

While in 1924, Christopher Obi was the pioneer catechist in Holy Ghost Church in Makurdi, the missionaries in Taraku were supported by Dennis Ahon Shaaji from 1945-1959, (whose duties as catechist extended from Taraku to Naka, and Gabriel Nyajo with Michael Aker served as mission cooks in both places). Patrick Uzuku, and Isaac Shom later served as catechists, and Sylvanus Alan, Lydia Ageenor led the way in Church music. In recent times, however, Thomas Ihula and Benjamin Udoh have served the parish as catechists in Taraku. When Naka was reopened as a parish after the Second World War, the parish was served by Peter Hwar from 1973-1975, Pius Tyo 1975-1987 as catechists, while Jeremiah Lough was the mission cook when the last expatriate, Fr. James Hunter CSSP left Naka to begin a new parish in Agagbe.[3]

Over in Udei, Michael Kinga Upaa was instrumental to the coming of the missionaries, supporting them to settle. Catechists

---

2 Personal interview with Fr Dominic Jir on July 13, 2021 at St Veronica's Parish Agidi, Mbatiav. Fr Jir oldest surviving Catholic priest of Tiv extraction at the moment. He was ordained in 1974.

3 Personal interview with Catechist Vincent Tartser on November 4, 2021 at St. Peter's Parish, Low Level - Makurdi. Tartser, who is currently the Catechist at St. Peter's Parish, previously served in Naka and Jimba as the Catechist.

Pius Jev, Innocent Bija, Michael Akuha, Julius Sough were among the earliest collators with the missionaries, while Donatus Abagi and Pius Akpe pioneered the efforts in liturgical hymns. Emmanuel Uiligh, James Iorzua, Samuel Togo, Francis Igbungu, Emmanuel Ikyo, Francis Ijeh, Jacob Bukem, and Benjamin Utsaha have all served Udei Parish as Catechists over the years.[4]

Indeed, Catechist Oliver Orkuma Kema of the old Abwa parish was an inspiration as I grew up in a mission church where the priest visited a few times a year. Catechist Francis Upav Tsegba continued that role in my life till I went to the seminary and got ordained as a priest. Tsegba died on the 30th of October 2021, after being sacked unceremoniously a few years ago, following over 40 years of service to the Church. Like many other catechists and church workers across Tivland, he was left to the mercy of occasional charity from Fr Emmanuel Asue and other kind-hearted people till death. May God rest him in peace. Amen. I cannot forget to mention Catechist Alphonsus Hembe and the voluntary catechists of the Mission Churches of St Joseph's Parish Akpehe in Makurdi, who formed me as a very young priest into who I am today. A record of the sacrifices of these saints across all parishes in Tivland should be kept.

The second reason is to call to mind how the Church as an institution in Tivland has fared in personnel management practices and the welfare of its lay staff, wondering if the Church can be "the light of the world" to our governments in this regard. Over fifty years ago, R. M. Downes, writing about the Tiv people, did say, "the Tiv religion was the basis of their social structure and of the moral code. . . The group acted in all ways as a unit."[5] Can the Catholic Church in Tivland, as an institution, approach general

4 Personal interview with Fr Dominic Jir on July 13, 2021.

5 R. M. Downes, *Tiv Religion* (Ibadan: Ibadan University Press, 1971), 5.

personnel management practices and the welfare of its lay staff as a unit to serve as a model for the government of the Benue valley at large?

As recounted in this collection, the Catholic Church has been phenomenally outstanding in ensuring access to quality healthcare and education in Tivland. The standards are enviable, from the Divine Love Catholic Girls' Secondary School Katsina-Ala, Queen of the Most Holy Rosary Secondary School Gboko, to Mount Saint Gabriel's Secondary School Makurdi. Healthcare services are legendary from Bishop Murray Medical Center Makurdi, Saint John's Hospital Gboko, to Saint Anthony's Hospital Zaki-Biam. These church institutions are functioning almost optimally well in an environment where disenchantment and poor working conditions constantly spark industrial actions by workers in similar government institutions, rendering them ineffective. Above all, the Church's response to the current humanitarian crisis arising from the displacement of many Tiv people from their homes by Fulani herders has been outstanding. From Anyiin, Chito, Jato-Aka, Daudu to Ukpiam, the internally displaced peoples' camps have been, for the most part, maintained by Church service organs like the FJDP, Caritas, and JDPC of the dioceses of Makurdi, Gboko, and Katsina-Ala, respectively.

While the Church must be commended for keeping the standards in its intuitions, and, not withholding the wages of its staff when due, it is not strange to note that most staff in Church institutions consider their work firstly as "service to God" before the consideration to earn a living. Like other churches, the Catholic Church also finds it convenient to base the bargain for the welfare of the staff of its institutions on the premise of "service to God."

Pope St. John Paul II, in his apostolic exhortation following the first African synod of 1994 *Ecclesia in Africa,* declared that "the main question facing the Church in Africa consists in delineating as clearly as possible what it is and what it must fully carry out, in order that its message may be relevant and credible."[6] Acknowledging the rapid growth of Christianity in Africa south of the Sahara, this document asks pointedly: "In a Continent full of bad news, how is the Christian message 'Good News' for our people? Amid all-pervading despair, where lie the hope and optimism which the Gospel brings?"[7] *Ecclesia in Africa* called for a religious imagination that can fashion concrete ideals to respond critically and prophetically to the restless desire for the advent of the reign of God in Africa, noting that "in Africa, the need to apply the Gospel to concrete life is felt strongly."

The general personnel management practices and the welfare of lay staff of the Catholic Church in Tivland is one area in our estimation that needs to evolve beyond the "service to God" rhetoric towards not just the attainment of the organizational goals of the Church but also the individual goals of the workers as people who earn a decent and just wage for their labours. In Nigeria, as is the case in most of Africa, the payment of the arrears of workers' wages that have been withheld for months is celebrated as an achievement, not an injustice. People are hired as government workers today and dismissed tomorrow by an incoming administration without any consequence. Parents and grandparents retire from service as government workers without any severance package with no pension nor health insurance after a lifetime of service to the State.

While the Church has been consistently outspoken in denouncing government failures in the treatment of workers, contemporary society finds absurd the authority of a gospel, upon which the Church stands, that sharply denounces every abuse of power, calling for the dignity of all of God's children, while at the same time not upholding a just standard for Church workers. What is the

6 John Paul II, *Ecclesia in Africa*, #21.

7 Ibid. #40.

policy for the employment, termination, and retirement of catechists, cooks, drivers, house-helps and other Church employees in Tivland? Are workers in Church institutions covered by any health insurance scheme as required by the laws of Nigeria? Are workers in Church institutions entitled to any pension upon retirement as required by the laws of Nigeria?

Just as the Catholic Church previously took on Roman and feudal structures, it has become clear that in our times, it needs to incorporate structures found in today's civil societies that are more compatible with the growing sense of our common humanity and that favour a fraternal community with the participation of the most significant number of people.[8] "Civil society has learned over the last two centuries that good governance calls for (1) the elimination of nobility; (2) the separation of powers; (3) the principle of subsidiarity (what can be done at a lower level of society should be done there); and (4) a system of checks and balances."[9] The Catholic Church in Tivland can draw from these to evolve a standard for general personnel management practices and the welfare of its lay staff. This will serve as a model for the government, just as the Church has already done in access to and the quality of healthcare and educational services over the years.

Besides calling for just welfare policies for workers in Church institutions in Tivland, we humbly propose that the Catholic dioceses in Tivland necessarily initiate a pension scheme for its workers. A pension is a portion of a worker's salary withheld to be paid to him after retirement. It is not a favour, but, in fact, one's earnings. Notably, we advocate for an insurance scheme for workers

---

[8] Gal 3:26-29: "You are one in Christ"; Mt 23:8: "You are all brothers"; Jas 2:2-4: "There must be no distinction among you."

[9] Thomas Reese, "Reforming the Vatican: The Tradition of Best Practices," in *Catholics and Politics: The Dynamic Tension between Faith and Power.* Eds. K. E Hayer et al., (Washington DC: Georgetown University Press, 2008), 216.

in the employment of the Catholic Church in Tivland, particularly health insurance. This will require the Church to pay little premiums to a health management organization so that the worker accesses healthcare at designated providers without a charge. Since the Church operates its hospitals, this can be effectively done at a very minimal cost.

It has been the practice that governments deduct from workers' salaries in the name of insurance and pension schemes, and politicians squander those monies instead of investing them, which results in no monies for salaries or pensions. The Catholic Church in Tivland can learn from the best practices of management sciences to evolve these schemes and operate them efficiently to serve as "light to the world" for the government to copy and give workers their due. This will be a significant milestone in the life of the Catholic Church among the Tiv in celebrating a hundred years of the encounter with the Catholic faith.

PHOTO GALLERY

First Church of St Joseph's Korinya Built in 1922

First Holy Ghost Church, Makurdi, built in 1926

Seminarians Dominic Yuhe
& Edward Maaer 1969

1971 Ordinands: Beba, Adzor, Yuhe, Ivever, Usuh, Adasu, Maaer

In 1996, on the occasion of the silver jubilee of the 1971 ordinands

CWO of Old Makurdi Diocese with their Chaplain on a visit to the Anglican Bishop of Makurdi 2007

A Cross-Section of Catechists In Tivland

A Cross Section of Church Leaders in Tivland

Bishop Usuh visits IDPs in Anyiin And Gbeji in 2001

MOST REVD
PETER I. ADOBOH
(First Bishop of
Katsina-Ala,
died February 14, 2020).

Bishop Avenya intervenes to restore the JS Tarka Stadium Gboko in 2021

Bishop Avenya leads clean-up Efforts in Gboko Town
to prepare for Christmas 2021

Bishop Anagbe Holds Peace Meeting with Women in 2020

Bishop Anagbe with some beneficiaries of his scholarships to IDP Children

CWO in front of the Holy Ghost Church,
the first Catholic Cathedral in Tivland

Some Tiv Catholic Choristers heading to a Congress
(This is still the reality of many of our members)!

Fr Moses Iorapuu

A Century of the Catholic
Church in Tivland
(1921-2021)

TEAM OF EDITORS

Fr Gabriel Wankar

Mr Joseph Eneji

www.ingramcontent.com/pod-product-compliance
Lightning Source LLC
LaVergne TN
LVHW010549160826
845677LV00013B/3062

* 9 7 8 9 7 8 5 8 6 9 5 6 9 *